Being Served:

Remembering 50 Luton Shops
of Yesteryear

Bob Norman

The
Book
Castle

First published September 2002
by
The Book Castle
12 Church Street
Dunstable
Bedfordshire LU5 4RU

ISBN 1 903747 19 8

Typeset and Designed by Priory Graphics, Flitwick, Bedfordshire
Printed by Impress Print, Corby, Northamptonshire

Photographs:
Front cover:
Evelings, Chapel Street
Back cover: *(clockwise from top)*
G.T. Osborn
Victor Furse
Evelings
W.A. Bloomfield & Son Ltd
W. Mooring & Son
Kamera-Mex

PREFACE

Bob Norman has produced a fascinating book. It is a most valuable contribution to the social history of Luton and at the same time a wonderful reminiscence for those thousands of Lutonians who remember the town as it was just a few decades ago.

The combination of words and pictures brings to life the old Luton, much of which was still to be seen in the 1960s and 70s. The book will give future historians a source of accurate information, meticulously researched and recalled by someone who grew up in Luton and spent his own working life in the town's retail trade.

Bob knew, and still knows, many of the families he records in his book, so what he has written is first hand and the more valuable for that. Bob Norman worked in the photographic business, and his photographer's eye has been used to great effect in providing pictures to illustrate the story of each and every local business covered by his book.

I arrived in Luton some 32 years ago, just after the heart of the old town had been demolished to make way for the Arndale Centre. At that time it was the fashion all over Britain to knock down and throw away the old, and to replace it with shuttered concrete, plate glass and multi-storey car parks. In a sense, we continued where the World War Two bombers had left off.

In Luton we lost two theatres, the Carnegie library and the whole of Waller Street, including the Waller Street baths. It was the era when we nailed plywood over beautifully turned banisters and handsome panelled doors, to make everything flat and flush, to look modern.

Nowadays we are doing all we can to preserve and restore the best of our older buildings, and thank goodness for that. We cannot recreate all that we have lost, but Bob Norman's book recalls with great affection and in loving detail some of the old Luton which so recently disappeared.

An awareness of a town's local history, both ancient and more recent, is essential to a community's sense of civic pride. Bob Norman has made a magnificent contribution in this respect and I take off my hat to him!

Kelvin Hopkins MP
Luton North

To Paddy
Mark & Peter
Sarah & Mandy
Daniel, Lindsey, Amy, Adam & Rosie

...my life.

INTRODUCTION

In 1776 Adam Smith said "To found a great empire for the sole purpose of raising up a people of customers may at first sight appear a project fit only for a nation of shopkeepers. It is however a project unfit for a nation of shopkeepers, but extremely fit for a nation whose government is influenced by shopkeepers." This phrase became accepted by our nation with pride, but since that time the diversity and individuality of our shopping habits have changed; we have less freedom of choice and our towns have become impoverished with the closure of many small shops. Census figures show that in the ten years following 1961 the number of small confectioners, newsagents and tobacconists dropped by 37%, grocers by almost a third, fruiterers by 27%, fishmongers by 24% and butchers by 16%. In 1973 alone, 455 pharmacies went out of businesss. Aggressive competition, universal branding and uniform packaging have robbed us of the service offered by the shopkeeper who could personally vouch for the quality of his goods. Let us hope, as we are increasingly affected by national advertising and more recently internet selling, that the personal service offered by the shopkeeper will not become entirely dispensable.

This book starts in the middle of the nineteenth century and reveals the stories behind some of the people and their families who were themselves behind the Luton names that could be lost in time if not recorded here, their important archive material being otherwise forgotten, mislaid or quite often destroyed. Most have never been written down before and many of the photographs have not previously been published.

Fifty stories tell of large department stores and of small corner shops. We have the chemist peering at you through the large coloured jars which shielded the dispensary filled with wooden drawers all with latin names on them; the barber with the red and white pole outside his premises; the baker who was always first to work in the morning offering bloomers, tins, split-tins, twists and cottage loaves together with that wonderful, freshly-baked smell and the tobacconist, usually a small personal business, providing also the smoking substitute, snuff. We read of those who sold books when essays, poetry and theology were amongst the best sellers; wine merchants who can recall when claret was 70p a dozen bottles; garage owners selling cars when it was the Morgan that gave you street-cred; music shops when flutes and mandolins were regular sellers and recorded voices spun at 78 rpm; shoe shops when they were made in the workshop on the premises; coal merchants offering a choice of cobbles, beans and nuts and not forgetting those who sold fleecy-lined pants, corsets and spring-steel trusses. Not all were shopkeepers, for we even have the stadium, the physio and the vet, but they all started from scratch with only an ideal and faith in themselves.

It was an immense pleasure to meet older members of the families and also their descendants who were so pleased to help with their innermost memories and family albums, happy to know that their parent's and grandparent's achievements will not be forgotten. Some were old friends, many are now new ones. They will all be remembered with pleasure, possibly affection, by the people of Luton whom they served so well.

Luton has changed so much in the past century, indeed in our own lifetimes. So many of the shops and services we remember have vanished that many of our subjects would not recognise today's high streets and shopping precincts. Although successful, it was the coming of the Arndale Centre to Luton which deprived us of many of our treasured buildings. John Betjeman was correct when he spoke of "planning authorities trampling on our hearts."

Many of you reading this book will, I am sure, be saying "do you remember..?", engaging in that pleasure enjoyed by most of us who are reaching the end of our warranty period. I speak of reminiscing, an activity once described as "the most fun an older person can have without actually having much fun." I hope you enjoy reminiscing with me.

Bob Norman

ABOUT THE AUTHOR

 Bob Norman was born in Leagrave, Luton in 1932. Educated at Norton Road Junior Mixed School followed by Luton Grammar School, he spent two years in the photographic department of "The Luton News" in Manchester Street, Luton. After National Service he rejoined Home Counties Newspapers at W. H. Cox in Wellington Street. Most of his business life was spent locally in retail photography as salesman, manager and eventually as general manager of University Cameras in Bute Street and later as manager with Lorell Photographics in Oakley Road. He is married with two sons and five grandchildren.

CONTENTS

AUTHOR'S NOTE

I would like to thank the large number of people who made this book possible by taking the time to talk to me and helping in so many ways. Also those who trusted me with their treasured photographs. Special thanks to my two sons who have assisted in different ways, but mostly to my wife who has been a tremendous help and encouragement on those days when I felt like giving up. I thank her for her continued love and support.

I publicly thank Janet Alexander, Eddie Andrew, Arthur Attwood, Ann Baldwin (AB), Bob Barker (BB), Malcolm Bass (MB), Doug Bloomfield (DB), Paul Bowes, Mona & Norman Booth (MNB), Elsie Buck (EB), John Buckledee, Jean Bullimore, the late Phyllis Burditt, Alan Campbell, Alan Cham, Philip Chapman (PC), Ron Coe (RC), Kathryn Cotterrell, M. P. Davies (MD), the late Doug Dennis, Jim Dockrill JD), John Edelnand (JE), Madeline Facer (MF), John Facer, Jean Farmbrough (JF), Stuart Farmbrough (SF), Derek Farmer (DF), Len Fay (LF), the late Irene Furse (IF), Stan Gordon (SG), Tom Haines (TH), Philip Harman (PH), Shirley Harris (SHa), Michael Harrison (MH), Mary Hay (MHa), Michael Henden (MHe), Kelvin Hopkins, Shirley Horn (SHo), Chloe Hucklesby (CH), Bryn Hyam, Molly Hyett (MHy), Ron Jeakings (RJe), Roy Joyner (RJo), Jane Lawrence (JL), Walter Lawrence (WL), Barry le Boutillier, John Lowden, Joan McIlroy, Joe McIlroy (JM), Betty McKean (BMc), Jean & Tom McPheat, Pip Manning (PM), Nick Marshall (NM), Edna Mills, W. Mooring, Bruce Moss (BMo), Bill Powers (BP), Bernard Ridgeley, Edna Rippengale (ER), Norman Saunders (NS), Wally Shanks, Sally Siddons, Diana Smith (DS), the late Ellis Smith, Eric Sutton, Doug Taylor (DT), Judith Thomas, Jean Thompson, John Thompson, Alison Thursfield (AT), Brenda Turnbull (BT), Michael Turner (MT), Wally Upton, John Walker, Roger Wash, John Watts (JW), Peter White (PW), Sidney Wild (SWi), Tony Wild, the late Ken Williamson, Peter Windmill (PW), Helena Wingrove (HW), Stephen Wolfenden (SWo).

Every attempt has been made to correctly acknowledge the photographs, the majority having come from the relevant families. If anyone feels I have failed to give them credit, I do apologise. Acknowledgement can be recognised from the initials shown above in brackets which are repeated underneath the photographs concerned. Some were "Luton News" photographs and I thank the Editor for permission given to use them here. Where no acknowledgement is shown and errors and omissions excepted, the photographs were either taken by the author or come from his collection.

Should the final result not have realised my hopes please, with my apologies, accept these words of Geoffrey Chaucer. "I beg them also to impute it to the fault of my want of ability, and not to my will, who would very gladly have done better if I had had the power".

Kenneth Bass & Son

It was graffiti, nothing more, just two words chalked on a piece of wood, but 37 years later it was to produce surprise and astonishment, and it's part of the Kenneth Bass story.

Lutonian Kenneth was born in 1907 in Cowper Street, the son of a local rural postman. He set up his upholstery business in 1932, using a hand barrow

Ken's name chalked on the seat board when he was an apprentice in the Vauxhall trim shop in 1929. (MB)

and a bicycle as transport, from a rented basement in South Street. Some of his early work was remaking mattresses, collected still warm in the morning, and delivered back in the evening ready to sleep on. A far cry from the world he was used to, having been apprenticed in the Vauxhall Motors trim shop, and later with Windovers of Hendon, upholstering the interiors of custom-built Rolls Royces. This was followed by a period in Southampton working on the great ocean liners, before returning to Luton and Vauxhall.

He showed admirable optimism and confidence by going independent during the economic slump. However, the quality of his work soon began to build his business, and he was able to make a move to 27 Mill Street. During the Second World War, Ken served in the Royal Air Force, but his wife Nellie, who came from Henry Street, kept the firm busy obtaining contracts to make BSA gun cartridge bags, and trim for the tanks and lorries being built locally at Vauxhall Motors and Commer Cars. After the war, seats were still made for Commer trucks, and the high-class upholstery and carpet work for the private sector returned.

In 1961, Nellie and Ken's son Malcolm joined his father in the business, and with soft furnishing a particular interest, a curtain workroom was set up in their new premises at 32 Waller Street, where their knowledge of modern and traditional curtain techniques brought further success. Their specialist work spread widely, from Luton Hoo and Luton Town Hall to London, including work in the Pavillion at Lords Cricket Ground, and in luxury Grosvenor Square apartments for middle-east sheikhs. Further contracts were achieved in the Isle of Man, Scotland, France and Switzerland.

In 1966 at the Vauxhall Heritage Centre in Park Street, a 1929 Vauxhall R-Type 20/60 Bedford saloon car was being stripped prior to being painstakingly restored. Originally selling at £495 it had now cost considerably more to bring it

Judith and Malcom Bass with the restored 1929 R-Type Vauxhall outside their Hazelbury Crescent premises in 1968. (MB)

back to Luton for display in the Centre. On the back of the rear seat board was chalked a recognized name....K.Bass! Later the senior vehicle restorer Bernard Ridgley drove the restored car to the Bass premises in Hazelbury Crescent where they had moved in 1968, a tangible reminder of the tradition of craft work carried on by Kenneth Bass & Son over many years. The photographs taken at the time are now a valued reminder of the past.

Malcolm Bass is a Fellow and past President of The Association of Master Upholsterers, and in this role has lectured to London students. He continued the family business after his father's death in 1981 until 1999 when he went into semi-retirement in Norfolk. The old Luton name of Kenneth Bass & Son is now partnered with that of the new owner Angela Burgin.

Kenneth Bass with Malcolm, age 10. (MB)

W. A. BLOOMFIELD & SON LTD
Bakers & Confectioners

Our subject produced, for almost a century, the most tempting smell on the streets of Luton.... that of freshly baked bread!

The original Bloomfields, Walter Snr. and Walter Jnr. (DB)

In 1890, Walter Bloomfield, whose father was a grocer, came with his wife Harriet from Ixworth in Suffolk and settled at 63 Stuart Street, Luton, later to become No.79 during the renumbering about 1925. They lived above their bakery using a coal fired oven from a side flue which needed constant and thorough cleaning. His brother Ernest also came to Luton at this time and opened his own bakery at 22 Hitchin Road. This year was also the first time Hovis loaves appeared in the shops.

The Bloomfield family were to serve the people of Luton for almost a century.

Walter Snr. takes his bread cart around Luton in 1918. (DB)

Their son Walter Athelstan was born, and carried the name of the Anglo-Saxon king who was grandson of Alfred the Great, probably to retain their Suffolk origins. He grew up to continue the family business and also the family tradition of devotion to the Methodist Church where he married Maud Cooper, making their home at 97 Dallow Road. Maud was one of the first ladies to be seen in Luton riding a motor cycle. On September 22nd 1962, at the age of 72, he officially opened the new Farley Hill Methodist Church in North Drift Way. The Revd. Brooker handed the key to Mr. Bloomfield saying "You are invited to open the door of the Church as a representative of one of the parent societies at Waller Street and as a Trustee of this building". To which he replied "In the name of Luton Methodists I open this door of Farley Hill Church". As there were so many people attending, tea for 300 was provided down the road at the Junior School. Their son

Douglas Athelstan had arrived in 1920, and a third generation was born into the trade of baker and pastrycook. In 1945 at the Waller Street Methodist Church, Douglas married Doris Brown from Bury Park Road. They made their home in Overstone Road, where they live to this day. Later, their sons John and Peter would become the fourth generation of Bloomfields in the family firm.

Douglas Bloomfield (DB)

Soon after coming to Luton, Walter Snr. gained the contract to cater on occasions

Peter Bloomfield at work using a peel to load the ovens (DB)

for the residents of the big house in Wardown Park, which we now know as the Luton Museum and Art Gallery. He also made and sold his own recipe of ice cream.

A second shop (now occupied by importers and exporters MK Brothers) at 273 Dunstable Road was purchased in 1963 and converted into a shop and bakery. This was forward planning prior to the closure of the Stuart Street shop, lost at the time of the road widening and building of the flyover in 1964. In 1967 a further shop was opened at 11a Upper George Street (now occupied by my son's company, Household Estate Agents). The Georgina Restaurant, later renamed Two's Company, was above and was reached by a stairway from inside the shop. During this time the company supplied Court Line and Britannia Airways, and also on the occasions of the visit of H. M. the Queen and the Duke of Edinburgh to Luton Hoo, Douglas baked them croissants and butter sponges made with pure butter.

Douglas recalls that at 5 a.m. he was usually the first to start work in the morning, but by 1 o'clock was regularly sold-out. This meant the start of the next day, with dough being prepared to stand overnight so that it was ready for baking the next morning. Public holidays and weekends could mean working around the clock, for sometimes triple the usual bake had to be prepared. Just one year short of their centenary, the company closed down on 4th February 1989, Doris and Douglas going into retirement with Douglas continuing his hobby of breeding tropical fish.

This "Luton News" picture, taken during the national bread strike of 1974, shows long queues forming outside the shop at 11a Upper George Street, Luton. (DB)

My wife who lived in Rothesay Road during the war years saw this story and immediately returned to her childhood! She said "Ooh, on Saturday mornings I would run down to that shop in Stuart Street for meat patties. I think they were sixpence, and we often had to queue for them. They were round and golden brown, I can smell and taste them now, they were delicious!" So Bloomfields the Bakers may have gone, but I am sure for many Lutonians, the memory lingers on.

The last cakes are baked, one year short of a centenary.

Blundell's

Blundell has been a family name in Bedfordshire and Northamptonshire for many generations, a Henry Blundell having been Steward of the Manor of Luton in 1225. The founder of the department store which is so well remembered in Luton was Henry Blundell, fourth son of Joseph Blundell who himself had a busy life in the Luton hat trade. Henry worked in the drapery trade in Preston and Newmarket before, in 1852, opening a small shop on Market Hill at the age of 18. It was between the Black Swan Inn and

The Cheap Clothing House, Henry Blundell's first shop on Market Hill in 1852.

Seabrooks, the corn merchants. He called his new venture Blundell Brothers because he hoped to have his younger brother

Thomas with him, but unfortunately Thomas died before this was possible.

As Luton grew, Henry Blundell's custom grew by working hard in his shop which had no official closing time, often serving until midnight. Three years on he rented, and later bought, a shop on the corner of George Street and Cheapside, this site to eventually become a very much larger store. A further five years later, buildings in Cheapside were purchased and rebuilt, making the original shop the furniture department. During the 1880s Henry bought more property in Castle Street and Chapel Street, and the Market Hill shop became the first in Luton to have a plate glass window. In 1887, Queen Victoria's jubilee year, Henry Blundell was elected Mayor of Luton having given long service in the public life of the town.

Henry Blundell

The 1890s consolidated the growing business and in 1902 Henry could look back on fifty successful years in business. The small shop of 1852 had become a department store of which he could be proud. The local press at the time reported "At Messrs Blundell Brothers establishment in George Street and Cheapside there is an exceptionally grand display. Both these large premises of business have been stocked and decorated for the Christmas season with a profuseness and magnificence seldom seen in the provinces. Indeed, the firm may be congratulated upon having saved

Blundell Brothers George Street premises in 1905.

first motor-van in 1909. With the end of the 1914-18 war shopping habits changed and Blundells with it, for the 1920s were the age of the short skirt and the shingle. It was also possible to furnish three rooms at Blundells for £50. The dining room cost £20-15-0 (£20.75) including a set of six chairs at £4-17-6 (£4.88). The bedroom came to £24-2-6 (£24.12½p) including an oak suite of wardrobe, dressing chest, washstand and chair for £13-5-0. (£13.25). The kitchen totalled only £5-2-6 (£5.12½p) which included a steel-top fender and irons for 12/- (60p).

the Luton public a very considerable sum in railway expenses, as it will now be quite unnecessary to visit any of the London emporiums".

A private company was formed in 1904 with Henry as the first Chairman and his three sons, Percy, Walter and Hubert as the directors. The Lamson Pneumatic Tube system for carrying cash from counters to the office was installed at this time, as was in 1906 the first customer lift. However, two setbacks also occurred. A fire destroyed the Market Hill premises, and in January 1907, Henry Blundell died. In addition to his business, he had served the School Board for eighteen years, and been a magistrate, councillor, alderman and Mayor. Under the control of the new Chairman Percy Blundell, the company prospered, buying their

Between the wars many improvements were made including, in 1928, the purchase of 10 George Street from Luton

The larger department store on the corner of George Street and Cheapside in 1928.

Corporation, two warehouses next to the Cheapside building and new modern shopfronts were fitted. In 1943 the company lost its second Chairman on the death of Percy Blundell, but he was succeeded by his brother Walter and a

furniture on the 'never-never', building up a large credit company, and later owning Dream Homes. It was he who, in 1955, took control of the Blundell stores but retained the familiar name to the public. In addition he controlled Fisks of

The Fashion Department on the first floor in Cheapside.

public company came into being in 1945. A Fabric Hall was made in the Cheapside store, and an interest taken in Blundell Rules Ltd., which made drawing instruments in a factory in Chaul End Lane. In 1951 the first floor in Cheapside was remodelled to form a Fashion Floor. The House of Blundell had become in 100 years a recognized shopping centre with 50 departments and a staff of 190. In addition to family members, F. J. Vine, T. E. Carpenter, S. C. Hayne, H. C. Cox and R. C. White had held directorships.

As a young man in the 1920s and 30s, Isadore Newton had toured the Newcastle area in a motor-cycle and sidecar selling

St.Albans and, in the early 60s, Merchants of Luton, and the Civil Service Stores in London's Strand, merging Blundells in 1964 into the Civil Service Stores Group. The Wesleyan Chapel in Waller Street became a Blundells store, and purely as an investment, a Pram and Cycle Shop also in Waller Street, managed for many years by Mr. Palmer, and also a similar shop in Dunstable. In 1965 Eveling's Dunstable Road shops became part of this growing empire.

In April 1973, Blundells became the major department store in the new Arndale Centre, doubling the size of their previous premises at a development cost of half a million pounds. At this time they claimed to be the only retailer, apart from a nearby market stallholder, to be selling hats in the town, despite the fact that Luton was traditionally the hat centre of Britain. However, success here was short-lived, and in January 1977 after 125 years, the name of Blundell officially vanished from the streets of Luton, as the company was sold once again to become the department store we recognize today, Debenhams.

A fortunate find of an album containing a few crumpled photographs tucked in with postcards of local interest at an out-of-town boot sale provided the pictures for this story. In addition my thanks go to Eric Sutton and Judith Thomas for supplying most of the facts contained herein. Eric was employed by Blundells as buyer of household linens in 1955, and became Store Supervisor. He stayed 19 years leaving to become Manager of Partridges in Chapel Street. He was also a President of the Luton & District Chamber of Trade, and now enjoys retirement in Lincolnshire. Judith, who still lives in Bedfordshire, also worked with Blundells; her late husband Howell starting work as a junior in menswear in 1950 and working his way up through several departments. He became manager of the fashion store in 1964 and a director on the opening of the new store in the Arndale Centre.

The furnishing showroom in the 1890s.

HANNIBAL BOND'S

The name's Bond.....Hannibal Bond.....licensed to sell!, and this he did with considerable ability and skilful business acumen for almost fifty years.

Mr. Bond was born in 1860 in Bishops Road, Paddington and was apprenticed to clothier Edwin Hewitt in London's Oxford Street, the site of which is now occupied by Selfridges. After a short time with Footman Prettys in Ipswich and Cobbs of Sydenham, he began his own business career at the age of 24 at Wells in Somerset. He remained there for fourteen years, and during that time married Sarah Dawson. In 1898 he moved to larger premises in High Street, Chiswick and stayed there a further fourteen years. However, with the coming of the underground railway and easy travel to London's West End, the high-class trade which he had enjoyed became lost, so in 1912 he made another move, this time onto Park Square in Luton. It was a bustling area filled with trams, horse-drawn wagons carrying hat boxes, market stalls and the occasional fairground ride.

Mr. Bond took over from Loomes, the drapery business at 19 Park Street founded by Mr. Kelly, the owner of the large Victorian property and already a good business concern. His enthusiasm led him to considerably enlarge his premises, to make alterations in the layout of the shop, and concentrate on a more working-class trade. With his family he lived above the shop for sixteen years

Hannibal Bond. (MHe)

Sale day in 1899 at Hannibal Bond's first shop in Chiswick High Street, London. (MHe)

Hannibal Bond's on Park Square in 1920. (MHe)

and corsets containing the best Greenland whalebone, some scientifically constructed for lady cyclists being cut low in the bosom and short in the hips.

Hannibal Bond's keenness continued right up to the time he was forced by illness to relinquish active leadership in the concern, after which the business was continued by his son Dawson and one of his daughters Queenie who was well-known as a prominent member of the

occupying the first and second floors, the third floor being for their servants and also some of the shopgirls who lived-in during the business week. At weekends they would go home, some to Welwyn and some to Toddington, on their pushbikes. Shop hours were long, sometimes until 11.00 p.m., and on Saturdays closing only after Mr. Bond had taken a walk to ensure that his competitors, especially Strange & Son in Wellington Street, had also closed for the day. The Park Square windows were crowded with displays of linens, wools, gloves, knickers, bras, combinations and corsets. There were fashionable art silk knickers with basque front; bras, or rather bust supports and bodices, laced at the back with pliable elastic to give free expansion for breathing; 'combs' in pure wool with high neck and short sleeves;

Interior of the shop in 1920 showing the departments offering curtains, corsets and underclothing. (MHe)

Luton Amateur Operatic & Dramatic Society. Hannibal took an active part in the trade life of the town, also enjoying fishing, shooting and the garden at his home "Mendip Lodge" in Cumberland Avenue to which he had moved in 1928. We know this today as Compton Avenue.

The Park Square shop finally closed in 1955, to become the premises of Pooles of Bradford who purchased the stock, and later became the radio and lighting dealers J. & F. Stone, before demolition in 1973. Hannibal Robinson Bond died at his home on 28th August 1935 leaving a widow, one son and five daughters. The funeral, and later that of his wife, was held in the place they loved most, the small Somerset city of Wells.

Hannibal Bond proudly drives his Wolseley motor car to the rear of his shop. (MHe)

Dawson Bond   *Queenie Bond (MHe)*

BONE & CO.

The musical instrument which originally came from Italy, and which had a deep almond-shaped body, was written for by some of the great composers, including Beethoven. That the mandoline, or mandolin, became very much part of our local scene during the last century was due entirely to the Bone family.

Phillip Bone was born in 1873, and lived in Bedford House on the New Bedford Road almost opposite The Moor

includes P. Bone in 1880. Phillip showed ability in musical subjects, possibly being a child prodigy, but surely his parents could not have known that he would become so famous and popular.

Shortly before the turn of the century he opened Bone & Co. in New Bedford Road, Luton selling quality musical instruments, soon becoming a national authority on stringed instruments, known in those days as fretted instruments. A feature of the shop was the musical doorbell which sounded very much like a few mandolin notes. Pianos, organs,

Interior of the New Bedford Road shop, about 1970.

in Luton. It is recalled that there were harps and harpsichords in the music room, and a harp on both sides of the fireplace in the living room. Old Bedford Road School, records several pupils named Bone, a common name in Luton, and

violins, guitars and mandolins were sold. Mandolins imported direct from Italy cost from 15/- (75p) to £12., and they were also the sole agents for Luigi Assano Italian violin strings imported from Naples, selling at 4d. and 6d. (2½p). An assertive

Bone's music shop about 1970, when the shutters declared "Instruments bought any condition".

which became a standard work in many countries. Phillip married Lily, having a daughter Irene and a son who lived only until the age of six. Lily died in 1926, aged 53, but Phillip remarried and had a second daughter Mary who was born in 1929.

As the children grew up, they naturally studied music. It was reported that Mary won the English Mandolinist's Championship at the age of 21. Irene became a member of her father's band and also an accomplished tutor. She was a gifted harpist who gave lessons to gentlemen's children in local stately homes including Luton Hoo, also played harp in London's Claridges Hotel, and performed with the London Philharmonic Orchestra. The Luton Mandolin Band held concerts all over Britain and locally at Round Green Methodist Church, the Central Mission in Midland Road and the band-stand in Wardown Park. A friendship was formed with the Excelsior Mandolin Orchestra of Holland, and joint concerts were presented in Scheveningen and in Luton's Chapel Street Methodist Church Hall. An eminent Dutch composer Jon Kok wrote a composition which he entitled "Lutonia" and which he dedicated to Irene Bone. "The Luton News" wrote "With the sweet slow melody to suggest the gently wooded hills and valleys of Bedfordshire, and the allegro motifs indicating the bustle and industry of the town, this piece of music has universal appeal. Surely there are not many towns in this country which can boast of having their very own music written for them by a leading continental composer".

Phillip continued to be a leading

advertisement in 1900 advised that their musical instruments were "not to be compared with those vile imitations made in Germany, and labelled and sold as Italian". Phillip conducted the Luton Band, and in 1890, formed a mandolin band which bore his name, becoming about ten years later the Luton Mandolin Band. He also published a book "Biographies of Celebrated Mandolinists and Guitarists"

The Luton Mandolin Band on stage in Scheveningen, September 1950. (BB)

member of the musical community and worked and played until his 90th year. Indeed he often kept his shop open until 10 p.m. After retirement in 1964, he died aged 91. Their family grave bears a sculpture of a mandolin. His daughter Irene decided to continue with the shop and kept it in the same condition as it was when her father was alive. She was reluctant to replace anything, even the gas lighting remaining for many years. Miss Bone was reported as saying that guitars were classical instruments and should be treated as such. She refused to handle or stock electric guitars, stating "they are only played by people who pretend to be musicians". Like her father she became one of the most respected and talented musicians in Luton, and in turn became the conductor of the Luton Mandolin Band. She played in South America, and often performed on the B.B.C. Home Service in the 'In Town Tonight' programme. Her father had been an adviser to the emerging film industry in

his time, and Irene continued this interest, providing soundtrack for the 1964 MGM film "The Yellow Rolls Royce". She also

The Bone family grave, regretfully now vandalised, but still showing the stone mandolin.

conducted a mandolin band at the British Federation National Competition held at Central Hall, Westminster, where she won first prize.

Irene Bone (she was in fact Mrs. Meeks but was always known as Miss Bone), died aged 84 in 1978. Her Steinway grand piano was left to a college of music in London. Luton High School girl Mary Bone, who had married a "Luton News" reporter in 1950, eventually retired to Scotland where she died about three years ago. As neither she nor Irene had any children, the Bone dynasty came to an end. The shop was finally sold, becoming first a hairdressers and later various other trades. However, the interesting green tiled exterior remains, depicting mandolins, drums and trumpets, all designed by Phillip Bone FRSA., and it remains a lasting memory to this exceptional family.

Luton Mandolin Band at 'S-Gravenhage, Holland. (BB)

BOOTHS of LUTON
for
POTTERY
CHINA
GLASS

BOOTHS

Although Mona Butters had Staffordshire parents, she had no real interest in pottery during her childhood, but she is certain that she was influenced by her grandmother who took her along to auctions around Lancashire and allowed her to bid for items from an early age. In addition, her friend's grandfather owned a large pottery warehouse in Accrington. "We played there for hours when we were children", recalls Mona, " and it must have left an impression".

After leaving Accrington Grammar School, she took up secretarial work with a weaving and bleaching company and in 1937 married Norman Booth, a Lancashire engineer who, after working at Leyland Motors and a spell in America, came to Luton and gained work with Vauxhall Motors. He was made welcome for his football ability, having played in the Lancashire Combination, and became a member of the Vauxhall Motors eleven. They lived in Runley Road.

Having saved some money, Mona and Norman decided they would like a shop, and that it would have to be china they were selling. The ringing of the cash till was in their blood, for both of them had been brought up in grocers' shops as children. However, the chances of Luton getting a new china shop looked pretty remote on the cold day in January 1946 when Mrs. Mona Booth trudged miles around the streets of Stoke in deep snow looking for a supplier. Several factories had closed during the war, stock was in short supply, and what there was had been snapped up by the big stores. It was a grim welcome for someone trying to start a new business. She spent a week there and sadly decided to return to Luton

In store display in the Bute Street shop in 1964. (MNB)

empty-handed. However, a conversation with an elderly gentleman on the return train helped, for he was Mr. Dean of Deans Teapot Factory, who gave her introductions to two other potteries. Mona jumped off the train at the next

The double unit at 43/45 Arndale Centre in 1972. (MNB)

stop, returned to Stoke and was then successful in buying and stocking the entire shop with £500 worth of pottery! That is how Booth's China Shop began on 21st March 1946, but then it was just the 12x10 ft. front room of a house at 67 Leagrave Road.

Soon a notice was going up on the door, "Gone to Stoke for more stock" and very shortly Mr. Booth also decided to take the plunge, and left Vauxhall to join his wife in the business. It was a gamble in those post-war days, with two young children, but things turned out well although at that time customers were rationed to three saucers, and cups were not always available! In 1947 they moved to a larger shop at Jasmine Parade in Leagrave Road, and introduced market stalls in Hemel Hempstead and Wolverton. Mrs. Gwen Spratley joined them at this time, becoming manageress and staying 25 years. The Booths were living near the shop at 23 Leagrave Road where their back garden went right down to Dunstable Road, and also using as a warehouse the big building put in the garden during the war for the use of the Fire Service.

A second shop soon followed at 30 Upper George Street, (now Apex House) when the Leagrave premises were vacated. The ground floor sold china and earthenware tableware, whilst the first floor displayed Pyrex ovenware and Cornishware for the kitchen. By the mid '50s, Booths were agents for Spode, Minton, Royal Worcester, Wedgwood, Beswick and Brierley Crystal, and by the early '60s, staff had increased to four. In 1962, with an understanding bank manager, a further gamble was made by mortgaging their house to enable a move to a much larger shop with a huge storage basement at 18 Bute Street, known as Bute House, and previously the premises of hardware and tool dealers Brown & Thomas. Their house was compulsorily purchased by Luton Corporation in 1966 to enable the building of Birch Link, the short road which connects Leagrave Road with Dunstable Road, so they moved to Haynes in Bedfordshire. In the same year a branch was opened in Welwyn Garden City which was successful for ten years. Smiles always greeted you at the door of the Bute Street shop; you knew immediately that it was a happy shop, and the impression was one of organized variety. Stock catered for all aspects of the trade but offered only what was good value, and they maintained a useful bride's

Mona and Norman Booth with the display of Royal Doulton china of which they were justly proud. (MNB)

book. Trade blossomed until 1965 when it fell off, due they felt to the introduction of parking meters in Luton, but they stayed here until demolition for the Arndale Centre reached them. In November 1972 a very fine double unit was opened in the new Centre at No's 43-45, used now by Dewhursts, the butchers. Four years later in October 1976, the final move was made to even larger premises at 107-109 on the main Mall, now the premises of Clinton Cards. This move was a mammoth job, taking all of a Saturday and Sunday with staff, husbands and children helping move convoys of stock along the mall using trolleys loaned by the local market traders.

It went on to become one of Luton's finest shops, offering the most comprehensive range of high quality china and glass in the south-eastern counties, and export of English china direct to customers was a speciality. A consignment of Denby stoneware to Japan is recalled by manager Alan Campbell, as is a traditional bone china dinner and tea service to a Russian gentleman who had called at the shop on a visit to this country. Two American customers are remembered; one from Pennsylvania came every year for 20 years bringing orders from his friends who also wanted English china, and another placed an order to supply him with in excess of 100 Wedgwood Blue Jasper

Christmas plates to arrive by November, for they were to be Christmas gifts to his staff. In 1960 your money would buy a 16-piece Meakins coffee set for £4/4/0 (£4.20) or a 21-piece Royal Doulton fine china tea set for £6/6/0. (£6.30). At the time of the royal wedding between Prince Charles and Lady Diana, Booths sold commemorative items to the value of £43,000. Mrs. Mona Booth went on to become national president of the China and Glass Retailers Association, and also in 1960, the first Lady President of the Luton and District Chamber of Trade. In 1981, with a promise of continued employment for existing staff, the business was sold to jewellers James Walker Ltd., who at that time had plans to open a number of shops combining china and glass with their own trade. However, shortly after the sale, James Walker were taken over by H. Samuel Ltd., who preferred to trade in jewellery only, and Booths was closed down. Clothiers Cecil Gee then traded from here for about eighteen months.

In retirement, Mona and Norman took a World trip, and liked best of all where their son Grahame was living. Although they have a great love of England, Norman's arthritis is helped a little in the warmer climate of South Australia, where they have settled. The Booths became expert in the china and glassware trade over 35 years in Luton, and a recently discovered coincidence is that many generations earlier, in Staffordshire, Mona Booth's family had lived next door to the Wedgwoods!

BROOKS (TYPEWRITERS) LIMITED

The pipe-smoking, always cheerful figure of Arthur Buck was well-known along Waller Street, Luton. His story, and that of Brooks Typewriters at number 16 on the corner with Barbers Lane, goes back many years. This type of business commenced here in 1926 when the County Typewriting Company took over from the plait merchant Abrahams. Five years later L.C. Smith & Corona Typewriters came into being, and this was managed by Harold F. Brooks.

Working with Mr. Brooks was young Elsie Cook from Dunstable who recalls that improving business in 1932 prompted the placing of an advertisement for a mechanic in "The Luton News", and Mr. Brooks asked Elsie to interview an eighteen-years old boy from Harpenden who had applied for the job. This she did, thought "he was a nice lad", and took him on at 25/- (£1.25) a week. The nice lad was Arthur Buck.

In 1939 they advertised "How irritating!...just when you have an important missive to type, your typewriter lets you down. This rarely happens with an L.C. Smith typewriter". They went on to say "greater efficiency in Luton offices has been experienced on the installation of

L.C. Smith smooth-running ball-bearing typewriters". In addition they offered "Corona personal writing machines in black and six beautiful colours for 21/- (£1.05p) down and 15/- (75p) monthly. Use it while you pay for it".

One day when Elsie was about to demonstrate a typewriter to a customer, Arthur whispered in her ear "If you sell that, I'll take you to the pictures". Encouraged by this, she made the sale, so off they went to the Alma Cinema, and romance blossomed. In 1939 Arthur was allotted shares in Brooks (Typewriters) Ltd., and in 1940 Elsie and Arthur were married at the Priory Church, Dunstable and set up home in the town. World-War 2 forced changes on the company when it became impossible to import the American machines. At this time Harold Brooks took over the business, and Arthur went off to serve in the Royal Air Force. A few years after the war Mr. Brooks died and Arthur became proprietor but retained the respected Brooks name.

Arthur Buck (EB)

Business prospered, selling adding machines, book-keeping machines, calculators, duplicators and dictating machines in addition to being agents for Olympia typewriters. Hayward-Tyler, the Davis Gas Stove Company and the local authorities were all good customers, and an efficient after-sales service department was maintained by Harold Petty and Ron Lyons.

As with so many local businesses, it all came to an end at the time of compulsory purchase to enable the building of the Arndale Centre. Arthur Buck decided not to re-open elsewhere. He worked for Staddons for a short time and later at Dunstable College until retirement in 1981. Arthur was a player with, and eventually President of, Dunstable Town Cricket Club. He also held the position of District Commissioner for Dunstable and District Scouts for ten years. He died, aged 68, in 1984. Elsie still lives in Dunstable.

Advert for Brooks Typewriters

Elsie Cook outside 16 Waller Street on the corner of Barbers Lane in 1934. (EB)

B. S. A.

Not the BSA you may at first have thought of, but it was a very important place to those who needed to go there. Bedfordshire Surgical Appliance Co, was in Stuart Street, Luton.

Ruth, who was born in Kettering, and Gerald Lawrence from Northampton, came to Luton in the early thirties when Gerald was working for an insurance company, and just before the outbreak of war in 1939 they bought the B. S. A. business. Gerald was considered to be in a reserved occupation, but he delivered wartime Vauxhall vehicles in convoy all over the country, and both he and Ruth volunteered for gas decontamination duty in the Civil Defence Service. Their children, Chloe and Paul, would sleep in the turkish bath rooms at the Waller Street Indoor Swimming Pool when their parents were on duty all night.

Chloe, now living in New Zealand, and I have recently renewed contact since our days at Christ Church Youth Club, and the next paragraph gives us her own vivid memories, through what she calls "the thick end of fifty years".

"No 36 Stuart Street was a small shop

Ruth and Gerald Lawrence (CH)

with a bow front and leadlight windows. The window over the shop at the front was also shaped in a shallow arc. The sides of the front were of brick, and there was a small step up to the shop door. Adjacent to the property was a block of relatively modern shops, including 'Norma's', a hairdressing business run by Norma Heck, and Maclaren Thompson's, a herbalist who sold all sorts of lotions and potions; then there was Spivey's, a small grocery shop. No's 38 and 40 were two small houses. Next there was Smith's Garage which also had a small grocery shop run by Mrs. Smith. Going back to beyond Spivey's was a large seed merchants called Byfields, and then the Duke of Wellington pub was on the corner. I believe the couple who ran it were Les and Ivy Woolston. My parents sold a wide variety of surgical appliances, including elastic stockings, elastic anklets, kneecaps and in those days quite a lot of trusses for men, some with elastic to go around to hold the pads, others were made of spring steel. They also sold made-to-measure surgical corsets and brassieres. Surgical boots and shoes and calipers were made to measure for shop customers and patients in hospital whom they used to visit in the wards or at regular surgical appliance clinics. Walter Mooring in

Wellington Street made some orthopaedic footwear for us. Occasionally they fixed up a customer with an artificial leg, and before the days of the N.H.S. they sold hearing aids. I recall an ear trumpet that was held in stock for years which was brought out for the use of a great-aunt who stubbornly refused a new-fangled battery operated Sonotone hearing aid when she visited us. We also sold infra-red health lamps and there was a large infra-red/ultra-violet lamp machine and a few people came in for treatment under this apparatus. When the blitz started in 1940 we moved into the shop premises to live, my father fixing up a bedroom in the cellar and we lived above the shop. This saved a certain amount of anxiety when the air-raid warnings went off, as the siren used to sound about six o'clock at night and as far as I can remember the all-clear didn't sound until morning. Just before the V1 rockets came into the war, we moved into premises on the other side of Stuart Street at No.61. To begin with we slept above the shop, which was later adapted to contain two fitting rooms. Greener's liquor shop was on the Wellington Street corner, then a confectionary shop run by Queenie Stocker and her mother. No.63 was occupied by George Ripper, a barber, the next was Deacon's jewellers, then at the end was Phillips newsagents. There was a narrow alleyway, then the Stuart Commercial Hotel, and the pub next door to this on the corner of Princess Street was the Duke of Edinburgh. The shop at No.36 was right opposite the Commercial Hotel which seemed to be very popular with the soldiers and their girlfriends. I admit I was too young to appreciate the reasons for their short visits, but it afforded my father considerable grounds for conjecture!".

Chloe worked in the shop from 1950 to 1957, but had married Jack Hucklesby in 1951. He was organist and choirmaster at Christ Church, Luton from 1947 until 1958 when they moved to Bournemouth, eventually emigrating to Auckland in New Zealand. In 1968, with Gerald's health failing into multiple sclerosis, interest in the business was sold to the Sheffield-based firm Ellis, Son & Paramore who transferred it to 20A Leagrave Road until about 1987.

The foundations of the shops remembered here are now under the road which forms the newer side of the dual-carriageway bordered by the Magistrates' Court. These were memories of a narrow Stuart Street which further back in the 19th century was described as "the lane leading out of Hog Lane into the Dunstable Waye".

BURDITTS BOOKSHOP

I regret that I am unable to remember Burditt's Bookshop at 47 Wellington Street. It was next door to Mooring's shoe shop, later became Jasons Mans Shop, and is now Josephs, the ladies' hairdressers. However, Phyllis Burditt, at the age of 95, wrote to me from her home in Cheltenham just before she died. I will reproduce her memories here almost word for word.

The business known latterly as Burditt's Bookshop was founded by my father Francis N. Burditt in the early 1880's (1883 I think), and in 1933 he achieved fifty years as proprietor and manager. By that time the burden was getting too much for him and I left my job in London to be his assistant. Eventually the tide of business traffic in Luton was moving eastward. Wellington Street was only on

the fringe and trade slackened so that we had to close the business. While it lasted it was a centre and rendezvous for many of the literary inhabitants of Luton who would foregather for discussions with my father and with one another about all kinds of books. On some days it was like a ministers' fraternal!

Francis Burditt. (AT)

There was a wide range of subjects stocked in the shop - fiction of course (but no pornography); biography; essays; poetry; theology; science etc., and books could be specially ordered. There were reward books too, for school and Sunday school prizes. I was allowed as a youngster to read any book I liked, provided it was returned in mint condition. That was a liberal education and it taught me to take proper care of books.

There were plenty of amusing incidents. On one occasion two girls in their late teens came bustling into the shop. They demanded "Have you got a book called "Les Miserables?" We thought it might cheer us up". I showed them a copy of Victor Hugo's masterpiece, and after looking at it they agreed with me that it wasn't likely to cheer them up very much, so they left without buying it. (They were almost illiterate!).

It was a grief to us when we had to close down the business, but I was always glad that we

47 Wellington Street, approx 1900. (AT)

Phyliss Burditt poses with her father in the shop doorway, approx 1930. (AT)

were able as a family to serve the community for so long ".

The shop closed in 1938, prior to the start of the second world war, but the building remained in the family until about 1980, being let to various tenants. Francis Burditt died in 1940.

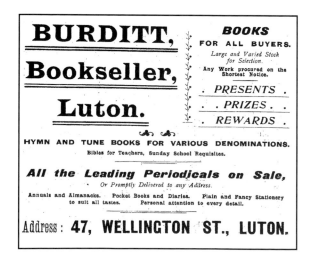

BURGESS
for
Minerals

In the middle of the 19th century, Luton was a compact little township with a population of 13,000 people, under 2,500 houses and less than forty streets. One of these was Langley Street, which contained a front-room sweet shop owned by Mr. James Burgess. When the straw-plait trade was good, his business flourished; but the hot days of late summer were not so good. Even the children who went to the British School nearby (two hundred of them attended for 2d per week per child) came in less frequently, and when they did it was for farthingsworths instead of ha'p'orths. Money was tight and in the really hot weather the confectionary lost its appeal, especially when thirst-quenching fruit could be bought on the market stalls. All he could sell was 'screws' of sherbert which his customers took home and used to make themselves delicious fizzy drinks. This made Mr. Burgess think!

He retired to a small shed at the back of his shop and started to master the art of making mineral water which was charged with carbonic acid gas. He produced the gas from chalk and acid, and also devised a hand-pump method of getting it into the

(left to right) James Burgess (Founder), Fred Hawkes (Foreman and first successor), Albert Hawkes (Son of foreman and second successor).

His way of creating consumer demand was to buy a wicker basket large enough to hold a dozen bottles, and tap on the doors of Luton businesses and shops saying "Try this!". He soon had to buy a rickety second-hand barrow, and later a larger one specially made for his business with "Burgess Luton Mineral Waters" proudly painted on the front.

One baffling problem he encountered was that when his bottles were stood up on end in the usual way, the corks dried up and contracted and the gas escaped. The drinks went dead because they didn't lie down. He took pride in his products and finally found the answer to the problem by compelling his customers to place their bottles of Burgess mineral waters in the recumbent position by means of a specially designed bottle. Just glance at the picture with this story.

Artist's impression of James Burgess's sweet shop in Langley Street.

bottles at pressure, spending all his savings in doing so. It was a tense moment as he watched the expression on the face of a sporting customer who tasted the first bottle of Burgess Mineral Water. The customer said "Ah!", and emptied the glass. That was enough for James Burgess who realised he was on to a good thing.

When James Burgess died, the firmly established business was taken over by his foreman Fred Hawkes, who bought a horse-drawn van for deliveries. After his death, his son Albert took over until 1907 when it was purchased by Mr. S. A. Attwood. Under his control, their Oxford Road premises were expanded (where the Dunham Mazda car show-rooms now stand on Park Viaduct) and before long five

Early morning outside the Oxford Road factory. (T.G. Hobbs)

horse-drawn vans were in use. In 1912 a newer factory building was commenced and a modern bottling plant installed, supplied by the local company Hayward Tyler. In 1913 Burgess' first solid-tyred chain-driven Commer two-ton van, reg. no. BM 3153, was trundling around Luton and the surrounding countryside. It was at this time that the company won four gold, silver and bronze medals for lemonade and ginger ale in open competitions at various exhibitions in London.

The first solid tyred chain driven Commer delivery van in 1913.

"They went dead if they didn't lie down!"

Between the wars Burgess developed into one of the finest mineral water factories in the Home Counties, having the combined characteristics of a modern dairy and a brewery. The scrupulous cleanliness gave it the resemblance of a dairy, whilst it resembled a brewery because of the interest of the employees in the firm's products, and they were allowed to drink as much as they liked. During the second world war, in 1942, the business was closed, machinery and transport were removed and the factory requisitioned by the Ministry of Food, whilst production of mineral waters was controlled by the Soft Drinks Industry (War Time) Association Ltd. In 1946 new machinery was installed, bottles and boxes acquired and a fleet of new vehicles put on the road. Mr. Attwood's son Arthur became the managing director and production continued until the early 1970s. From this time forward the company progressed into the early 1980s concentrating on supplying soft drinks to local shops and the licensed free trade in South Bedfordshire and Hertfordshire. At this time he was joined by his nephew John Facer who took over the day to day operation of the company. It continued to expand, concentrating its efforts on the licensed free trade by distributing draught and bottled beers to its established

One of the later large fleet of delivery vehicles.

customer base. As the company progressed into the 90s, recession hit smaller companies and changes took place, restricting distribution into the licensed trade. A decision was eventually taken to close the doors and all assets were sold in 1991.

Little did James Burgess know when he ventured forth into Luton from the little Langley Street shop with his first basket of bottles, that his name would thereby live on for more than a hundred years, and become a household word in South Bedfordshire and the neighbouring counties.

The last word in Bottle Washing.

Buttons of Luton

Button Brothers came to Luton in 1905, but curiously this is something of a misnomer. There never were any brothers! There was only ever Mr. Alfred Ebenezer Button.

Born in 1883 at Forest Gate, London, it was he who decided to call his first business venture by a name which was to become a household phrase in Luton and for miles around. It was clear that to get on in Luton you had to appear well-established and give an impression of

Alfred Ebenezer Button.

solidity and a good bank balance. Mr. Button, being a prudent young man with sufficient capital provided by his father Ebenezer, felt that the introduction of this imaginary brother into the style of his firm added at least another "0" to his capital in the eyes of his customers. It was not just one man starting up, but a firm .....
Messrs. Button Brothers.

He opened in a small single-fronted shop at 11 Park Square on Saturday, 28th October 1905 at an annual rent of £80. The takings for the first week were just over £5, but the next week was slightly better and a growing and loyal clientele was gradually established. His father, Ebenezer, who became Company Secretary, was quite a difficult man to work with. Even after his retirement to Herne Bay, he continued to audit the accounts and was known to complain that new string had been used to parcel up the books, wanting to know what was wrong with the old pieces of string!

It was not long before Alfred had to start looking around for bigger and better premises. He found them right in the middle of George Street at No. 44 in the shape of a lock-up shop on the corner of Bond Street, a one-time busy private road and a short cut to Barbers Lane. Bond Street, which was barred one day every year to preserve its

Button's first single-fronted shop at 11 Park Square in 1905. (TH)

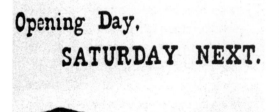

Open on Saturday Next,

OCTOBER 28th.

BUTTON BROTHERS,

11, Park Square, Luton,

FOR GENTS

New Hats,	New Gloves,
New Ties,	New Collars,

New Fancy Vests,

New Umbrellas, &c, &c.

Opening Day,

SATURDAY NEXT.

Cutting from "Luton News,"
October 26th, 1905,
of the opening announcement

Luton News Advert.

drawn from the hat trade, including the names Burgoyne (later Sir John), Sanders, Shoosmith etc., and Mr. Ebeneezer Button was the first Chairman.

Then in 1919, just across the narrow tramlined main street, the building opposite at the bottom of George Street West became vacant. These premises at No. 53 were promptly acquired and, when

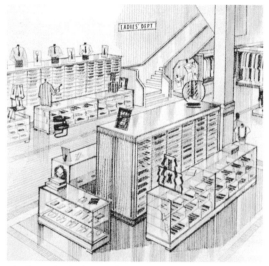

The design for the layout of the ground floor of the shop in 1937. (TH)

all the alterations were completed, the new shop was the smartest showpiece in George Street until one day in 1933 when a dray horse bolted across George Street from Bond Street into the front of the shop, damaging the framework. The horse had to be destroyed.

In 1923, Mr. A.J. Shreeve and Mr. A.H. Akhurst joined the Company and were later invited to become Directors. Mr. Shreeve managed the Ready-to-Wear Department and Mr. Akhurst became Manager of the Harpenden Branch which had opened in 1922. Mr. Tom Haines joined the firm in 1934 having served an

owner's right, was blocked for all time in 1954 when fishmongers MacFisheries built a branch shop on the George Street end. Alfred's new shop, well fitted out with fine woodwork and a new front, was the home of Button Brothers throughout the first world war. It was about this time that the business became a private Limited Company, the first shareholders being

apprenticeship with Percy Raven of Southend-on-Sea and in 1945 was appointed to the Board. Mr. Roy Button, son of the founder, became a Director in 1936 and joint Managing Director with Mr. Haines in 1947. Later Dr. Jack Burgoyne (son of Sir John), became the Chairman, combining this job with being a consultant scientist.

There was much talk of a badly needed street widening scheme for George Street, it having undergone a startling change over the past 20 years. The numerous hat factories had almost all moved and it was now a fully developed shopping centre. As part of this the council purchased the property, setting back the new building line, the Savoy Cinema (later the ABC, and now vacant) being built on this site. Following a closing down sale which went on for many days, with long queues forming and the shop having to close for meal breaks, the final Button Brothers premises at 41/43 George Street were opened in 1937 on a 49 years lease. The first artist's impression produced for a brochure showed the new shop front with a car parked outside. This had to be altered to show clearly that it was a Vauxhall.

World War II made its impact when, on the 1st September 1939, Buttons were given two hours notice to clear their large basement for immediate conversion into an air-raid shelter for 200 people. There was a sand-bagged entrance and later a concrete blast wall, so window displays became pointless. With utility cloths, austerity suits and clothing coupons, there was little to put on show. A man needed to save 26 coupons, about half his annual allowance, for a suit (jacket 13, waistcoat 5 and trousers 8).

It was a very personal business, with customers treating the staff as friends. The gentlemen's "barber shop" with five qualified staff and a chiropodist, attracted men from many miles around, but the Chairman did not approve of it and never went in. A shave, with hot towel and hairbrush, cost 6d (2½p), a shampoo with radiant heat was 8d (3½p) and face massage or violet ray treatment were each costing 1/6d (7½p). The Vauxhall supremo at that time had declared that no-one was to leave the factory for shopping outside of lunch breaks, but was embarrassed, when doing so himself and calling for a hair cut, to find two other Directors there for the same purpose. In 1954 a highly successful fashion parade was held in Luton Town Hall, with audiences of over 250 at each showing. Bespoke tailoring was an important part of their business, the casual flipping through the pattern book, the leisurely inspection of the cloth between finger and thumb, the discussion of personal preferences; buttons? vents? slanted pockets? There were complete display areas for hats and caps, hosiery, gloves and ties, dressing gowns and "hosts of pyjamas in sleepy patterns", and not forgetting the ladies' tailoring.

After 73 years that most delightful and rewarding of shops, which kept in step with the times, was sold to Fairdales in 1978 who retained the Button Brothers name but later sold it on to Moss Bros. The building now houses the Bonmarché shop. Roy Button is retired in Leighton

Artist's impression of the new shopfront at 41/43 George Street in 1937, with the Vauxhall car parked outside. (TH)

Buzzard, and Tom Haines in Kinsbourne Green, near Harpenden. Mr. A.E. Button, "the Guvnor", retired to Southbourne and died in 1968. He said with true modesty that "the family business was part of the English way of life. It catered for, and was appreciated by, folk who looked for the finer things in life". Button Brothers said they always offered something for the well-dressed man to wear, "apart from a flower and a smile".

Coventry Radio

Before the First World War, 191 Dunstable Road, Luton was a private residential house, known simply as "Meadowcroft", but this area was soon to become commercialised and lose its rural ways, Chibnall & Clutton being the first in business at No. 191. In 1925 it was here that Maurice Napp, who had previously traded from his shop at 36 Castle Street,

The Coventry Company at 191 Dunstable Road in 1925. (SG)

opened the Coventry Company, selling bicycles and accessories. It was because the bicycles he sold were produced in

Coventry that the firm got its name. Maurice had three sons, Ronald, Leonard and Eric and all three joined their father in the business. Radio station 2L0 was only three years old when this company became established as specialists in the supply of radio components, but these were the days of crystal sets and cats whiskers and headphones placed in a bowl to enable all the family to hear. When the sale of these products became greater than sales of bicycles the name of Coventry Radio came into being. During the war years radio components became almost impossible to obtain and very few new radios were available in the shop, so a five-valve radio chassis was designed and made in their workshop, which filled a very big need.

Prior to this time, David Gordon had a successful electrical business with his brother in London, but in 1940 David came to Luton. With his wife Lillian and their three children they lived at 864 Dunstable Road, and opened their own company, Radio Electrical Services. Later they worked at Coventry Radio, and in 1951 the Gordon family were able to take control of this business. Daughter Gladys became company secretary, and sons Keith and Stanley were instrumental in the company's progress. In the early 50s some of the first high fidelity amplifiers were made in their own workshops and they were the first local firm to demonstrate tape recording techniques. The family also recall that it was one of the first shops where the enthusiast could experience at first-hand the original Leak valve amplifiers and Quad acoustic

The larger premises in 1965. (SG)

loudspeakers. In 1973, at the age of 73, David Gordon died.

One night in September 1980 disaster struck when a fluorescent light failed, causing a plastic sign to melt, resulting in a devastating fire which destroyed both stock and premises. Tragically, the care taker, who lived above the shop, died in the fire. The company rose again from the

The scene of absolute destruction in the shop after the fire in 1980. (SG)

ashes, when they rebuilt and were appointed stockists of many of the big names of the day, including Grundig and Bang & Olufsen. The company supplied equipment to colleges, schools, factories and government departments at home and abroad. An independent family business in an industry dominated by multiples has a difficult task, but Coventry Radio were effective and competitive in Luton for 57 years, the name finally disappearing when closure came in 1982. It is now the premises of Bargains Galore.

Stanley's sons David and Jonathan were also part of the business between 1973 and 1986, but in October 1978 they had opened Technosound on the gallery of

(left to right) Jonathan, Stan and David Gordon. (SG)

Luton Arndale Centre, one year later in the Milton Keynes shopping centre and seven years later a third branch in Dunstable. The Luton branch closed in 1994, but Jonathan still offers a personal service to the discerning hi-fi enthusiast, now in the Willen Local Centre at Milton Keynes. To date the Gordon family have been in the radio trade for 76 years. Stanley and his wife Valerie are now retired in Dunstable, and Keith and his wife Brenda live in the Buckinghamshire village of Northall.

Harry W. Covington lived and worked at his tobacconist's shop at 5 Cheapside, Luton from the beginning of the 20th century. It was one of the first shops in town for all those interested in smoking, but the choice of retailers of cigars and cigarettes increased rapidly from this time. These shops had a unique smell all their own, often accentuated by the stocks of aromatic snuff. Business remained in his hands until 1926, when it became Harrison Tobaccos Ltd. but retaining the respected name of Covington.

Frederick George Harrison was born the son of a Salisbury chemist in 1902. His wish was to become a jockey, but he grew beyond the required size. After schooling he became apprenticed to a manufacturing tobacconist, and later gained further experience in his chosen trade, working for Offers who were retail tobacconists in The Arcade in Bournemouth. Although this is now the designer clothing shop Gabucci, an elegant polished brass sign on the premises still informs passers-by that it was once the home of Offers, the cigar importers. Whilst in Bournemouth, he met his future wife Beatrice Smith.

George Harrison in 1920. (MH)

George, as he chose to be known, was only 16 when his father died, the legacy from the sale of the chemist's business being held in trust until he was 21. In 1926, having consulted a business broker, he was offered two suggested purchases of the type which interested him, one in Luton and one in Wimbledon. He decided on Luton and purchased Mr. Covington's shop in Cheapside, for which he paid £2000.

George's cousin, Nathaniel Simmonds, also opened a similar shop in Bedford High Street which is still trading as Harrison & Simmonds. George and Beatrice lived at first in Farley Hill and later in the newly-built Wardown Crescent, where they had two children Michael and Joan.

Harrison Tobaccos Ltd., trading as Covingtons, became a premier shop for all who wanted to smoke tobacco in its many forms and

The crowded window display at 5 Cheapside. (MH)

in various ways, and of course for those interested in taking snuff. Kegs containing 14lbs of snuff, which was sold in very small quantities, would last for two months. All the finest products from the big national companies were stocked. There were Dunhill, Barling and Dr. Plumb pipes. Gold Flake, State Express and Abdulla cigarettes. J. S. Salome, Couronne and Wills Whiffs cigars. A whole range of accessories included Pullmatches, Ronson lighters, tobacco pouches and jars, pipe-racks and cases, wooden spills and pipe cleaners, smokers cabinettes and even Wilkinson and Rolls razors. They advertised in 1939 that they were "Luton's largest retail tobacconist".

Michael and Joan Harrison behind the counter at 5 Cheapside, about 1955. (MH)

Having a lifelong interest in horse racing, and being an account holder with local bookmaker Mr. Lancaster, George was a useful contact for staff at the nearby shops and market who wished to place bets in the days before betting shops were available. On Derby days this could mean more betting activity than tobacco retailing, and sometimes the bets would not be 'laid-off' to the bookmaker, but 'stuck' in the expectation that an unfancied horse would win. A coterie of older gentlemen often gathered in the shop to place bets and discuss racing, including Colonel Rattigan, father of playwright Terence Rattigan, who lived in nearby Pepperstock. Well known customers of the legitimate business were pipe-smoker Eric Morecambe and cigar-smoker Tommy Cooper.

In 1953 a new light-oak shopfront was made by shopfitters W. H. Hudson of 21a Chapel Street, at a cost of £500, and this was also the year that George's son Michael joined his father in the business. Michael stayed eight years before emigrating to New Zealand with his wife Hilary. The names of both Covington and Harrison departed from the business life of Luton at the time of compulsory purchase in 1973. Together they had served the town's smokers for more than sixty years. Much of the shopfitting was sold off; the author was recently shown in a private house a beautiful wall cabinet which came from the shop, now displaying porcelain and also elegant tobacco jars decorating the windowsill. F. G. Harrison died in 1981. Michael Harrison became a successful manufacturing jeweller in Hamilton, New Zealand, and his personally made jewellery is also on sale in a gallery in St.Albans. He and his wife chase the sun by living in Hamilton for four months, and in Harpenden for the remaining eight months of every year.

CROMWELL GARAGE

Close to Epping Forest, in the Essex Borough of Wanstead, in April 1908, Wilfred James Rippengale was born to a printer and his wife. Young Wilfred was bought up a very strict Baptist child in a God-fearing Christian family, so it was

W.J. Rippengale..."Rip". (ER)

understood that Dad had refused an offer of work with 'The News of The World'. From a very early age the little boy didn't like being called Wilfred, and became known to all as Rip. Both the name and the Christian values were to remain with him all his life. Rip's Father wanted him also to be a printer, but when he left school at 15 other interests surfaced and he was, at this age, the only boy in his school able to build a radio. For 15/- (75p) a week his first job was as a junior

in a retail radio shop, and then as manager of a shop in Chiswick at the age of 20, progressing to Southampton Row in central London.

This is the point where the family became local to us, moving to the Bedfordshire village of Little Brickhill, and in 1930 Rip married Kitty. He first managed a radio shop in Bedford, but in 1934 moved to Currys radio shop at the corner of Smiths Lane in Luton. He always believed that he sold the first television set in Luton, and at this date it is quite possible.

During the war Kitty became an ambulance driver, and with his mechanical abilities Rip was soon asked to do the necessary engine repairs, very often having to make parts which were not at the time available. He eventually became driving instructor and Station Commander of the wartime ambulance posts at Beech Hill, Dallow Road and Park Street. He also lectured in local factories on anti-gas measures, protection against high explosive bombs and incendiary bomb control for the Luton Air-Raid Precautions Scheme under the authority of the Borough of Luton Police Force. In the peacetime of 1945 he decided it was time to go into business on his own. Renting a private garage in Ascot Road, he worked long hours repairing motor vehicles, enabling him to open Cromwell Garage in Cromwell Road in 1948. It is here that he will be most remembered, for he gave honest and efficient service for 29 years until his retirement in 1977. His policy was never to take on more than he could manage so that the quality of his service

Cromwell Garage. (ER)

known as The Golden Gleam when it raced at Brooklands, and was earlier owned by Jimmy Nervo of the Nervo & Knox Crazy Gang team. Rip sold it on, via dealers Henlys, to Mr.Carol Griffith Jnr. who purchased it to export and add to his collection of Jaguar cars at his home in Delaware, U.S.A. When in the United States recently, I spoke with Mr. Griffith who recalled at length the pleasure that DDV 777 had given him. Although he has now sold his collection, he assured me that this car is still running well, and valued by another owner.

In 1968 Rip remarried at Luton Register Office. His bride was Edna Waller whom he had first met whilst mending a puncture for her. Edna came from well-known local families. Her grandfather

did not suffer. He even held a list of prospective customers whom he refused to serve until he had "a slot" for them!

In 1951, for the sum of £585, Rip purchased an unusual car, SS-100, registration no. DDV 777. Standard Swallow, abbreviated to SS, was one of the early forerunners of the Jaguar marque. It had low-slung good looks with a long louvred hood, high gull-wing bumpers and deep bucket seats. With Jaguar's new overhead-cam 3-litre engine, true 100 mile-an-hour performance was realised. By reason of its rarity it became easily recognized in the area. I recall being given a demonstration of its abilities along New Bedford Road, Montrose Avenue and Biscot Road, an exhilarating if uncomfortable ride. Although now in metallic green, it had previously been

Rip at the wheel of the SS-100. (ER)

was in the hat manufacturing trade, and Uncle Herbert was High Sheriff of Bedfordshire at the time of the Queen's Coronation. Edna taught at Denbigh Road Junior School and later became Deputy

Head at the William Austin Junior School. In Rip's retirement, and with Edna at his side, their interests blossomed. Together they studied and collected antique furniture, 18C drinking glasses and Minton porcelain. From an early age Rip had an interest in astronomy, building small telescopes. With tremendous help from his friend Horace Dall, an acknowledged expert in optics who lived in Luton, and also from mechanics at George Kent Ltd., he built, in his garden, a 10" equatorial Newtonian electrically driven reflector telescope. His photographic work with this instrument led him to give a lecture on its use to the British Astronomical Association. It is still in

Sir Patrick Moore OBE.

private use in Keysoe, Bedfordshire. The Cromwell Road premises are now occupied by Optikinetics.

Microscopy also figured large in his interests, saying "You can look into the sky and see the hand of God, and also into the microscope and see the same wonders". Rip, an extraordinarily interesting man, died in 1993, aged 85. Edna still lives in Luton with her two sisters, Phyllis and Edith. At the time of Rip's death, internationally respected astronomer Dr. Patrick Moore O.B.E. wrote to me saying "I am sad about Rip. I liked him a lot. He was a superb astronomical photographer, and a splendid companion with a marvellous sense of humour".

The low-slung good looks of Rip's SS-100. (ER)

D. R. DENNIS

Our subject was born in, schooled in, worked in, formed his own business in, and lived until his recent death in, just one district of Luton. Douglas Raymond Dennis was born at 125 Marsh Road, Leagrave, Luton, in 1919, almost opposite Day's the newsagents and cycle shop.

69 Grange Avenue, Luton in 1966.

Mum was a Luton girl, but she married a carpenter from London whom she had met during WWI when he was stationed at the Biscot Camp in Luton. They were married at the Holy Trinity, Biscot Parish Church. Douglas attended Norton Road and Denbigh Road schools and was a paperboy at Freddy Day's, who was his Uncle. Leaving school at 14, he worked at Alf Williams's wireless shop along the road, mostly charging the acid accumulators which were necessary at that time. The next job was as a trainee carpenter where his father worked, Davis Estates Ltd., who were building the houses in Willow Way and River Way. The third job came with cabinet maker and coachbuilder William Kiddy at 148 Old Bedford Road, Luton, until the outbreak of WWII. Douglas was conscripted into the Royal Engineers, but had to be discharged after receiving an injury resulting from a lorry accident in the north of England. The rest of the war was spent at the Electrolux factory in Oakley Road, Luton where war contracts involved the manufacture of road bearers, shells and depth charges.

Peacetime of 1945 brought a change of employment into the planning department of the Percival Aircraft Co. at Luton Airport, but two years later he entered the trade which was to become the rest of his business life. Doug became a radio engineer with the Derwent Radio Co. situated on the corner of Stuart Street and Wellington Street, but personally covered the Letchworth and Baldock areas. In 1953 at Biscot Parish Church, the Rev. Shewring married Doug and Londoner Margaret Burke who was living in Beechwood Road, Luton. They set up home in Orchard Way. Two more jobs yet before the final one. Doug became manager of Wilson TV Rentals in Upper George Street, and then had an unsuccessful venture, opening, with a friend, a radio and television shop in Flitwick.

The significant year for Doug was 1962 when he rented 69 Grange Avenue in Leagrave and opened his own radio and electrical shop. Main agencies of Ultra, KB,

Doug Dennis in his crowded shop in 1966.

Philips, Dynatron and Echo were appointed and business was good. In this small shop Doug and his wife were taking £1,000 a week, a very rewarding figure at this time. Stocks of lamps, batteries and cables of all types filled the narrow shelves. The counters and window were full of fans, doorbells, radios and televisions; and as technology advanced, video recorders as well. Behind the shop, in his crowded workshop, Doug would repair anything electrical, and also undertook electrical contracting. The shop was always so full of new and serviced stock, it was sometimes difficult to get in further than the doorway, and also for Doug to use his vintage wooden cash till on which on the roll of paper contained therein he would manually record each sale in pencil. Enthusiasm waned after the death of Margaret in 1992, but their busy shop in Grange Avenue had offered good service to customers far beyond Leagrave for 38 years, finally closing in 2000. Doug retired in Leagrave, and enjoyed membership of the Masonic Club and the Lansdowne Club. His other interest was classic cars, and he was still driving his 21 years old Morris Marina until his death in July 2001.

If it's for your Pets –
DOCKRILL'S
– If it's for your Garden

I wonder how many female readers of this page can recall in their younger days hearing a wolf-whistle as they walked along Dunstable Road, Luton. Of course it may have been genuine, but it is also possible that

Jim Dockrill (right) aged 14 with A.J. Pearce at his shop in Lea Road, Luton in 1933. (JD)

Jim Dockrill. (JD)

it came from outside the biggest pet shop in town where a beautiful green parrot was well-known for turning the heads! Luton has seen many fascinating shops, but few can have been more exciting in its day than Dockrill's which attracted hundreds of children and their parents to gaze upon the fish, birds, rodents, reptiles and animals.

Jim Dockrill was born in Henry Street, Luton in 1919, the son of Ralph and Millicent. For a short time they lived in a hut in the garden of 84 Dunstable Road, then in a flat at the same address and later in Ridgway Road. He attended St. Matthews and Old Bedford Road schools, and after failing to get a job with Webb Brothers the gents outfitters in Bute Street, joined A J. Pearce as an assistant at his garden and seed shop in Lea Road. In Dunstable Road, No.84 was grandfather's house where a small sweet shop occupied the front room. This is where, in 1937, with grandfather's retirement and a £100 loan from an Uncle, Jim opened his own pet and seed shop at the age of 17. At this time there was just a grassy bank opposite the shop, for the Odeon cinema and adjacent shops were yet to be built. The war years were spent in France and Germany serving with the Irish Guards Armoured Division, during which period his mother kept shop for him. She lived in Stamford Road and would daily cycle to work from her Round Green home. She lived to be 98 years old. As business improved, a move was made into the larger shop next door at 82 Dunstable Road, which had previously been occupied by Emily Blown and her sister, selling babywear.

In 1963 someone walked into the petshop and literally got the bird, for Polly Dockrill the chattering parrot went missing, believed stolen, for it couldn't fly,

The original Dunstable Road shop. (JD).

voucher at a dog show to spend in the shop. "I bought some Good Boy chocolate drops with the voucher, and by the time I reached home I had eaten the lot!" he said.

Son David, cousin Roy, Joy Brooks and many others worked at the shop and Jim looks back with appreciation for the good service they gave and the friendship they enjoyed. Regretfully Jim's wife Dilys was unable to help, as she had an allergy to animal fur. In 1979 when he closed down, and insurance brokers Robert Rushton converted the premises into their own, Jim Dockrill brought to an end a period of what is now nostalgia to Luton, and many of the town's residents still recall with affection the happy memories they have of the shop. Customer Joyce Catchlove of Beresford Road wrote

having no flight feathers. Polly had appeared on ITV nature programmes and left behind a sad colleague George Dockrill, a grey parrot. Luckily Polly was found fluttering about on Dunstable Downs by a Barton man, who cared for it until he learned where it had vanished from. It chattered away when it got back but not a word about where it had been, nor how it got to Dunstable. Following alterations to the shop, radio "Zoo Man" George Cansdale officially opened the new top floor display, and Jim often assisted local wildlife expert Graham Dangerfield with his television shows.

Lutonians queued at Dockrill's to buy goldfish, mynah birds, parakeets, guinea pigs, kittens and puppies. In the garden department where they were expert seedsmen and bulb importers, wonderful tomatoes came daily from the local Putteridge Nurseries. But not everyone spent anything. Some just visited out of curiosity - it was just like going to the zoo. One customer recalled winning a 7s.6d

Jim with little room to spare in his shop in the 1960s. (JD)

"What will we do without Dockrills... I cannot comprehend... Do you think the Queen is aware... That an era is at an end?"

EDMA *Jewellers*

Success in business was very sweet to John Edelnand because the story of his early career was bound up with the tragedies of war that in his case placed him as a refugee in a strange country at the age of 14. He was born in 1924 in Halberstadt, north of the Harz mountains in the Magdeburg district of Germany where his father had run his own jewellery business, and arrived in England just one week before war broke out in 1939.

After spending his first week in Britain under canvas in Ashford, Kent, he was moved to North Wales where he worked on a farm. "I had learned some English at school" he recalls, "and my first opportunity to try it out was near the farm where I worked. Unfortunately my choice was a poor one. An old man to whom I spoke replied in Welsh, the only tongue he knew. No-one had told me that Wales even existed, let alone had a different language". But life eventually took a turn for the better when young John moved to Leicester to live with an aunt and following his father's trade, started work with H. Samuel as an apprentice dealing with customers. "I left them for a while" he remembers "to take a job as a waiter at the Conservative Club, just to get enough money to buy myself a new wardrobe". Then it was back to the trade with

John Edelnand

jewellers George Waterhouse to begin training on craft watch repairing, which was to eventually earn him the honour of Crafts Member of the British Horological Institute. Soon his talents brought him promotion as manager of Tennants in New Bedford Road, a branch purchased in Luton by George Waterhouse of Leicester.

1948 was an important year, for in Ashby-de-la-Zouch, he married Maisie Bent. They had met in Leicester at the home of a mutual friend. In the same year he followed in the family tradition and initially opened his own business in a first-floor workshop above McIlroys Travel Bureau in Waller Street, specialising in the repair of watches and making parts for jewellers all over the country. There was a demand for this work as the country's workforce was not

John was Manager of Tennants in New Bedford Road. (JE)

John's first retail shop in Mill Street, Luton. (JE)

re-established in the immediate post war years. With a modest workforce of principally Austrian craftsmen, retail premises were now acquired in Mill Street where Maisie and John lived over the shop. The business name EDMA was formed, the derivation being an amalgam of ED from John's surname and MA from Major, the name of a partner with whom he worked for only a few months. In addition to the growing watch and clock repair and manufacturing work, the retail side sold only clocks, watches and accessories at this stage. Jewellery items were not introduced until 1951.

Although he still undertook some of the more complex work at the bench, much of John Edelnand's time was taken up building the retail side of the business, looking after customers, buying, selling and administration. Eventually a shop assistant joined the staff as the jewellery side of the business became established, and promotions such as the Engagement Ring Week brought in new customers from the town and rural Bedfordshire. It was in the days at Mill Street that Edma introduced its own brand of watch - Texina. They were imported from Switzerland, and spot checks were made by stripping one movement from the range to determine quality, before being sold under the house name.

In 1950 a move was made into a more central shop at 20 Cheapside, investing in more staff which, in addition to a large workshop still staffed by many of his original Austrian craftsmen, now included a manager and four assistants.

A compulsory purchase order on Cheapside forced a decision in 1972 that

The large Arndale Centre shop in 1972. (JE)

John and Maisie at retirement in 1983. (JE)

took Edma into the Arndale Centre and to a position of prominence in the town. John's natural optimism took them into Unit 10, which was the largest then available at the Centre, sporting no less than thirteen six-foot windows in its 100ft frontage.

The business, now the largest independent jewellers in Luton, flourished and continued to expand throughout the 1970's, but "one good branch was quite enough to handle" says John "and we never thought at any time of opening others". Having no children of their own,

John Edelnand and his wife Maisie, who played an important active part in the business since its conception, began to think about what in the long term would be the best direction for the business to take. In 1979 the highly successful business, Edma of Luton, was sold to the James Walker Group, an acquisition they recorded at the time as one of the largest and most exciting made. John Edelnand continued as Managing Director of the company he had built so successfully, but finally retired in 1981. The story went full circle in 1993 when H. Samuel, who had purchased James Walker, closed the shop, for this was the company with whom John had started as an apprentice. Maisie and John enjoy their retirement, but John still admits to missing the challenge of business. He has been a member of Luton Rotary Club for over thirty years, and a founder member of the Edelweiss Club. He organized and acted as Master of Ceremonies at many 'Oompah' fund-raising events in aid of the British Heart Foundation, the Luton Pasque Hospice and many other charities. The Edma premises in the Arndale Centre are now occupied by Vodaphone and Massarella's Mall Cafe.

Edma Arndale Centre shop staff in 1972.

EVELINGS

Let's really look back into the past... to the year 1897. In those days Luton was almost entirely dependent on its flourishing hat trade. Vauxhall, Commers, Skefko and Electrolux had not yet thought of coming to Luton. However, an ambitious young man working as an assistant at Charles Mares shop, at that time on Market Hill, was busy saving his wages. It took him some time to save £30, but decided that this sum would be sufficient to start up in business on his own.

That young man was Thomas Kerridge Eveling, born in 1871 at Whitstable in Kent, where his father was also a clothier. With his £30 capital he opened his first shop at 1 and 3 Chapel Street, investing every penny in merchandise and boxes. By the time he had packed his window with his stock of clothing and hats, and hung an impressive quantity outside, there was very little to go on the shelves. He had bought many cardboard boxes from local hat box makers, so he labelled them ties, socks, caps, etc placing them on the shelves, although empty of any stock. It looked impressive and when a customer enquired to see something, he would lift

Thomas Kerridge Eveling. (JW)

the box down, remove the lid and looking surprised that it was empty would say, "My goodness, I must have sold them all!". His bold show must have puzzled established outfitters, but his prices were keen, and the business prospered to such an extent that within a year he decided to distribute some restrained and dignified publicity in the form of a small card which is shown on the next page. The dignity of the premises was occasionally lowered, for the slaughter house was behind the premises and on occasions the flock of sheep being moved down Chapel Street would go astray and enter the shop, only to be herded together and out of another door.

The shops were affectionately referred to by most Lutonians either as "Everlings" or "Evlings", but the correct pronunciation of Evelings is "Eevlings". When goods were delivered to Chapel Street by the railway horse and dray in the early 1900's, the regular driver would invariably announce his arrival by calling out "More parcels for Everlean and Neverfat"!

It seems clear that the shopping public of Luton increased their patronage, for within a few years Mr. Eveling, ably assisted in the shop by his wife Miriam (née Whiting) whom he had married at

Linslade Parish Church in 1899, acquired the lease of adjoining premises, vacated by Carpenters shoe shop, and which were some of the oldest buildings in the town.

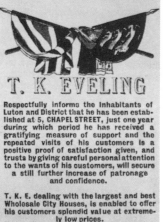

Eveling's publicity card of 1898. (JW)

This enabled the extending of the sales of men's and boys' clothing and outfitting, ladies' and children's outfitting and general drapery. Now operating from 1,3,5, and 7 Chapel Street, he also befriended C. W. Turner at 37 Wellington Street who was not doing as well as he, and for a short period took over this shop as well. Older Lutonians will remember Mr. Eveling with grateful pleasure, for it was always his custom and delight, for he loved children, to present any youngster with a small birthday gift on production of their birth certificate.

Twelve years after commencing trading, Albert John Watts was taken on as an assistant, and his salary was increased to thirty shillings (£1.50p) per week when he got married. The business was formed into a limited company in 1935 when he succeeded Mr. Eveling as Managing Director and later as Chairman, eventually giving over sixty years service before retirement. In 1946 when Mr. Watts' son John joined the company following army service, expansion plans were severely curtailed by wartime restrictions, clothing coupons and rationing which still persisted. So a decision was taken that John should open a separate shop for the sale of toys, baby carriages and nursery furniture. The premises taken at 145 Dunstable Road, to the right of the Odeon Cinema, had previously been used as an air-raid shelter, with a bomb blast wall on

Eveling's staff on their stand at a local exhibition. (JW)

The shop at 1 and 3 Chapel Street, Luton. (JW)

made history by providing Luton's first roof-top car park. Other branches on short term leases were in Wellington Street, Leagrave Road, Dunstable Queensway and a corner shop in Stopsley managed by Gaius Rollings who at one time also ran a country round making sales from his van.

LuDun Ltd. the Bedfordshire workshop for the severely disabled which was in Liscombe Road, Dunstable, were always grateful to Evelings and to John Watts in particular, for it was through them that the LuDun range of toys was placed on the market. Evelings helped with designs of the toys and a new limited company, Luton Toy Co., was formed. Originally it operated alongside the Evelings retail business, but due to rapid growth, wholesale distribution was moved to Inkerman Street. Success was maintained, and the

the pavement outside. It was opened without a proper floor, shopfront or fixtures, and the toys were displayed on army trestle tables. However, it was soon firmly established, so much so that within five years plans were commenced to make the Dunstable Road unit "Eveling's -The Children's Store". At a cost of £40,000, the five shops in this parade became 7,000 sq ft of selling space with 100 prams on display, the latest electric train sets, an 18ft long exhibition of dolls and the best nursery furniture and bedding. It also

Eveling's children's store in Dunstable Road, Luton. (JW)

Albert Watts (left) and John Watts. (JW)

the company to Blundell Brothers in 1965, and Luton Toy Company was sold to Leighton Stationers in 1968. The Chapel Street premises are now occupied by Gladrags and Storage, whilst the Dunstable Road unit houses Funky Junction and the Shalamar Tandoori Restaurant. John continues to enjoy his retirement with his wife Pauline at their home in Harpenden. The ladies' and children's wear departments continued until 1977, when they closed due to the expiration of the lease. Thus Evelings completed 80 years of trading in Chapel Street.

company exhibited at the 1955 British Industries Fair.

Thomas Eveling died at his home in Ludlow Avenue in 1940, and Albert Watts died in 1969. John Watts sold his part of

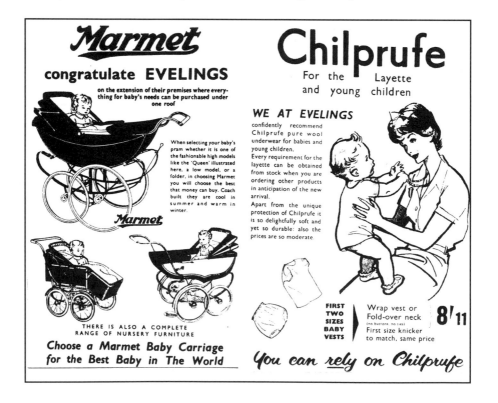

JOHN FACER & SONS

The family name of Facer appears in Bedfordshire records in the mid 1600s, and it is believed that they came here from Northamptonshire, their professions at that time being similar, i.e. manual workers or farmers, in both counties. A further point to consider is that the name of Facier is an old French family name and quite a large number of French people settled in the Northamptonshire area, the French Court having sat at Fotheringhay Castle in the period 1400-1600.

Our subject here is the third son of John Facer of Houghton Turn, Dunstable who was born in 1851 and also baptised John. At the age of 14 he entered the straw warehouse of Mr. George Elliott in George Street, Luton, but after four years forsook the straw for the coal trade.

He joined Messrs. J. Cox & Son of Bute Street, remaining with them until he was 28, leaving only to set up as a coal, coke, salt and brick merchant on his own account with premises at 54 and 56 Cheapside through to Guildford Street, Luton at which he also lived. On Christmas Day in 1875 he married a Dunstable lady Miss Mary Young and over a period of years they had ten children. John was a tenant of the Model Farm in the Luton Hoo estate for 21 years and they later lived at " Llanstephen" in Hart Hill, Luton.

John Facer took a leading part in the establishment in Waller Street of the local Friendly Societies' Medical Institute in 1889. At that time he had been an Oddfellow for 20 years, a member of the Industry Lodge of which he was secretary and later senior trustee.

The founder, John Facer. (MF)

Although never contesting a seat on the Town Council, for as one of the Council contractors he was ineligible for membership, for some years he sat on the Board of Guardians. He also sat on the House Committee of the Bute Hospital and was a Deacon of King Street Congregational Church. He often assisted in the big demonstrations which used to be a feature of the Bute Hospital appeals in the closing years of the 19th century and also had happy memories of field days at Luton Hoo and Putteridge Park.

The slogan "Facers for Fuels" became synonymous with quality and good

The offices at the corner of Cheapside and Guildford Street. (MF)

"Daisy", one of Facer's carthorses pictured in 1941. (MF)

service; horse-drawn vehicles (and much later diesel conveyors) delivered coal, coke and anthracite throughout Bedfordshire and Hertfordshire. Forty years ago coal was available in many forms. Facers sold cobbles, cubes, cobs and nuts, and the cost was eleven shillings (55p) a hundredweight, a saving of 6d (2½p) per cwt. being possible if you ordered eleven cwt. in one delivery. Best anthracite could be ordered as French or boiler nuts, stovesse, beans, grains or Phurnod, which were Welsh nuts. Brand names of Coalite, Warmco and Rexco were available as smokeless coal, and also Sunbright hard coke was sold. In 1900 they advertised that they held the Luton and district agency for Hodgen's Finest Big Vein Anthracite which was used for malting,

hop drying, lime burning and horticultural and steam purposes. The best hard steam, colliery nuts, slacks, tanfield, foundry coke, gas coke and breeze were marketed. Indeed all domestic, commercial and industrial requirements could be met and truck loads delivered to country stations came at colliery weights. Facers held the Coal Utilisation Council diploma. Premises were also held at 168 Dunstable Road, at a depot in Leagrave Road opposite Tudor Road and a coalyard was kept in the grounds of the Bute Street Railway Station. In early days the delivery horses were kept in the yard to the rear of the company offices on the corner of Cheapside and Guildford Street. This remained their public order office for the whole of Facer's century of business life in the town centre of Luton from 1879 to the early 1980s.

John Facer's sons Sydney and Alfred were responsible for the continued success of the family business after the death of their father in 1929. Sidney Bennett, George Newbold, and A. Powdrill were present at the funeral, as well as representatives from J. T. Byfield, Charles Franklin and Brentnall & Cleland,

Alfred Facer Jnr (left), and Sydney Facer (inset). (MF)

showing the respect that the entire local coal trade had for John Facer. In the meantime Sydney married Tessa Holding and Alfred married Edith Rudd.

During the second world war Sydney's youngest son James and Alfred's son Alfred Messenger Facer both served in the RAF. Jim was the Flt. Lt. Commander of an air sea rescue boat and Alfred was on ground crew servicing bombers, and for a time serviced Grp. Capt. Leonard Cheshire VC's own aircraft. In the peacetime of 1946 they both joined the company and became directors, gradually taking over from their fathers and forming the third generation in this local family concern. However, their fathers still kept a watchful eye on the business.

In the 1950's Facer's took over the coal business of R. Dudley of 1 Ashton Road, Luton although during this time solid fuel continued to be strictly rationed. The government Fuel Office was in Upper George Street, opposite the Town Hall. The Bute Station coalyard was partly mechanised with hoppers in the 1960's and the business also diversified with a paraffin delivery service. A fuel oil agency was introduced, supplying to industrial customers such as George Kent Ltd and to many nurseries. Facer's were the first local coal merchants to use Charrold conveyor sack delivery vehicles. As we move into the 1970's, the National Coal Board opened a large mechanised coal depot in the Leagrave Road premises which was to be used by all merchants in the area. Jim and Alfred were asked by the NCB to run the depot for them, so by this time the Bute Station depot had become redundant. Alan Cham, who had joined the company in 1954, now became Manager and remained with Facer's for the next 24 years. Chartered accountants Mitchell & Plummer occupied the first floor in Cheapside for many years. The 1970s also saw the advent of cheaper gas from the North Sea and with it the coal trade began to decline, this period seeing Facer's delivery lorries reduce from 19 to 5. However, this was also the time that Facer's took over the coal business of Sidney Bennett. About 1975, the distribution business of John Facer Ltd.

was sold to British Fuels Ltd., which was itself a subsidiary of the larger Amalgamated Anthracite Holdings Ltd., a nationwide group registered on the Stock Exchange.

Jim retired and moved to Norfolk, where he had boating interests at Wroxham and, later died there. Alfred Jnr. who had been a prominent local magistrate, retired from the running of the Leagrave Road depot in the early 80s, and he also died later. Alfred's family are still in Luton, and in Harpenden James's son and two grandsons continue the family name.

The Luton building is now the office of solicitors Gordon Young, but their polished brass letterbox still reads John Facer & Sons, Coal Merchants.

The black solid opaque substance that we know as coal was once the basis of modern industry. It cooked our food, lit our homes, weaved our clothing and kept us warm. The past century saw its importance rise and wane, and that pattern was reflected in the great success and eventual decline of the Luton family coal business that was John Facer & Sons.

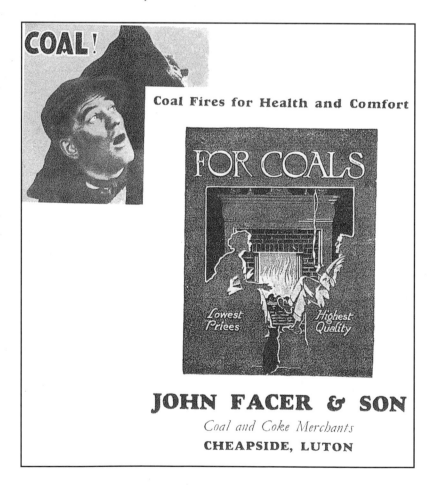

Molly Fardell

The veterinary surgeon has been important in society for many hundreds of years, veterinary science being said to have begun in the Egyptian civilisation, and the Romans left writings on the subject. In modern times, however, the most important function of the veterinary surgeon is all aspects of animal husbandry, and in private practice the 'vet' is called upon to deal with all kinds of animal suffering. During the last century small animal practice became very important and some vets, especially women, became almost wholly engaged in it, which is where our subject fits in. To many residents of Luton, and far beyond, the name of Molly Fardell became synonymous with skill, experience and compassion in her chosen profession.

Molly was born an Eastender in Leytonstone, London but the family came to Luton in 1943 when her father was appointed manager of the Luton Co-operative Industrial Society dairy at 1 Manor Road, but later opened his own dairy in Burnham-On-Sea. Molly was educated locally at Moorlands School in High Street, Leagrave and for two years at Luton High School for Girls in Alexandra Avenue. However the move to Somerset meant completing her education at Bridgewater High School. In fact due to wartime evacuation she attended eleven different schools, eventually qualifying as a veterinary surgeon in 1957 at Bristol University. She worked with Arthur Goddard in Wanstead, London until

January 1st 1960 when she purchased the small-animal side of the established practice of Powell & Wilson at 1 Brook Street, Luton on the corner with New Bedford Road.

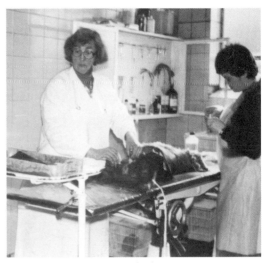

Molly at work in the new operating block in 1962. (MHy)

In May of that year, in Colchester, Molly married shoe manufacturer Alan Ernest Hyett, and they moved into The Old Rectory in the Bedfordshire village of Lower Gravenhurst. Their family of Stephen and Sarah were born there, and they also successfully bred Border Terriers and Irish Wolfhounds. The Brook Street practice went from strength to strength under Molly's resolute determination and vigour, often seeing 35 animals on a Saturday afternoon and another 45 on Sunday. During the '60s some assistants at the surgery became well-known to Luton animal lovers, especially Elizabeth Rogers, Linda Driver and Eddie Andrew who specialised in dog training and trimming, and still has her own Luton dog parlour today. Molly had a phone-in advice spot

No. 1 Brook Street just prior to demolition. (MHy)

Brook Street when, in 1988, the practice was sold to Peter Kembell. Molly said at the time, "It's very sad but it has been marvellous. I couldn't imagine ever doing anything else. I'll miss my clients and their animals very much. I have been through several generations of animals with many of them". Her staff described the practice as a "a whirlpool of emotion". The building was eventually demolished, but in new premises it remains Icknield Veterinary Centre.

Molly and Alan retired to live at Lanzarote in the Canary Islands, where sadly Alan died in 1998. However, you can't keep a good vet down, especially Molly, for she still practices on the island, working as a vet for "Pals", and helping with their monthly charity fairs. In addition she gives up her spare time to raise considerable funds for The Amigos of

on Chiltern Radio and also appeared in naturalist Graham Dangerfield's weekly TV series. Police work was important, as was helping the British Wild Animal Collection. For her services as an honorary veterinary surgeon to the Luton Canine Association, she was made a life member in 1988.

Molly's husband Alan was elected a Councillor for Luton Icknield Ward in the local elections of May 1966, and served the local community for five years. He was a member of the Housing & Planning Committee for four years, and its Chairman for two. He became an Alderman of the Borough in 1971, but didn't quite make it to be Mayor. Molly laughingly says "I was quite looking forward to being chauffeured in the mayoral car, but I was unsure about kissing the babies at election time!".

Molly and Alan semi-retired in 1987 but, after 28 years, the brass plate bearing her name came down from the surgery in

Molly at retirment in 1988. (MHy)

Lanzarote, a charitable society she founded which helps people who are in trouble, as well as looking after their animals. Car boot sales and an annual dance are organised. At retirement Molly Fardell B.V.Sc., M.R.C.V.S., received this poem from her staff included in a red book entitled "**Molly & Alan This Is Your Brook Street Life 1960-1987 - Ten Glorious Years**".

To be a successful and competent vet, needs knowledge exceedingly wide,
For each of their patients she's likely to meet, possesses a different inside.

She must know why the cat is refusing her milk, why the dog is not eating his bone,
Why the coat of the horse is not shining like silk, why the parrot does nothing but groan.

Why the ducks and the chickens are failing to lay, why so faint the canary bird sings,
And if she is called to the zoo she must say an incredible number of things.

If the lion's got a cold, if the zebra's getting old, if the centipede has trouble with his feet,
If the hippo's feeling ill, if the bison's got a chill, if the arctic fox is suffering from heat.

If some virulent disease has attacked the chimpanzees, if the tortoise hasn't stirred for years,
If the bear's too full of buns, if the cobra eats her sons, if the panther's wife chews his ears.

If giraffes have had a tiff, and their necks are feeling stiff, if hyenas don't laugh at keepers jokes,
If the monkey's pinched his tail, if the rhino's looking pale, if the elephant eats bags and chokes.

If the camel hurts his hump, if the kangaroo won't jump, and if the crocodile won't bite,
They run away and get that omniscient, the vet, and expect her to put everything right.

Profoundly I pity the vet who must learn such a very great deal for her pay,
My son, I advise you most strongly to earn your living an easier way.

Don't attempt to attend the zoological crowd, a far more reasonable plan,
Is to call yourself 'doctor' and so be allowed to specialise only on man!

CHAS FARMBROUGH
Everything to furnish the Home

In the tiny village of Old Bradwell, Buckinghamhire, now part of Milton Keynes, Charles Septimus was, as you may have observed, the seventh child born to Charles Griffes Farmbrough and his wife Marian on 18th January 1885. The family moved to Dunstable where, at the Priory Church, he met Ida Mabel French. She was aged nine. Ida moved with her family to Sevenoaks in Kent, where her father became a successful dairyman, but in 1922 Charles was also in Sevenoaks and this time for his marriage to Ida. They set up home in Lansdowne Road, Luton, for Charles was already in business here.

After trade training in London and further experience in Aldershot, it was in 1911 that Charles had bought the established household furniture business previously owned by William Wren and his Son at Park Square. Next door were ironmongers and engineers W.J. Barrett, and on the other side lived Charles Irons, the Town Crier. Mr. Farmbrough modernised the premises and held a clearance sale of the entire stock, announcing that he "while wishing to retain the confidence and support of all the old customers, hopes by careful and prompt attention to business to gain many new ones". Later he took over the ironmonger's premises and built extensions to the rear. Rooms above, once used as living accommodation, became storerooms. There was a well in the basement which they covered and the

27 Park Square, Luton in 1911. (SF)

entire floor lowered to provide a carpet store. He built up his trade as Charles Farmbrough, the Cash Furnisher with the principle of payment "on the nail". He never gave credit to his customers, and asked for none from his suppliers. No goods were delivered to customers on the obscure promise "Mum's out, she'll pay you when she comes back!" They advertised that they were the only house furnishers in the town doing an exclusively cash business - no booking charges - no bad debts to allow for -

therefore lower selling prices. Furniture at this time would have mostly been in dark wood. This was fashionable as well as dark carpets, dark curtains and dark wallpaper.

With the coming of the first world war, 29 years old Charles Farmbrough advertised "Having decided to respond to my Country's call, I beg to inform you that I have joined His Majesty's Forces, and shall be away from business for an indefinite period. Arrangements have been made for the business to be carried on during my absence, and I trust you will continue your support during that time, overlooking any little inconvenience that may arise out of the special circumstances. I take this opportunity of thanking you for past favours and hope that in the near future I shall be fortunate

Charles Farmborough. (SF)

in renewing my acquaintance with Luton and receiving an extension of your patronage". He served as a Lieutenant in the Bedfordshire Yeomanry. His brother Oliver, previously an apprentice watchmaker with E. Deacon & Sons of Wellington Street, handled the enterprise during the war. For many years a branch was operating at 203 Dunstable Road, and eventually sold to furnishers A.C. Rivers.

After 45 succesful years trading in Park Square, retirement came with the closure of the business, when in 1956 the entire row of shops was demolished to make way for extensions to the Luton & South Bedfordshire College of Further Education, now the University of Luton. The value of the goodwill was lost, only a disturbance payment being made.

The enlarged premises 25/27 Park Square in 1930. (SF)

Charles and his family lived in Old Bedford Road, where he died in 1973, aged 88. His two sons, Stuart and David, are also well-known in this area. Stuart was a Luton based chartered surveyor and land agent; also a Justice of the Peace and Magistrate, a member of Rotary Club in Luton and a President of Luton & District Chamber of Commerce. In 1984/5 he was the Queen's legal representative holding the position of High Sheriff of Bedfordshire. His wife Jean, a former head girl of Luton High School and former head almoner at St.Albans City Hospital, is the daughter of Godfrey Osborn whose story is told elsewhere in this book. They are retired and living in Pavenham, north of Bedford. David progressed in the Anglican Church, being ordained a priest and becoming a curate at Hatfield, then Vicar of St.Michaels at Bishops Stortford, and later Archdeacon of the diocese at St.Albans. Finally he was Bishop of Bedford for twelve years before retiring to Bromham in 1993.

Farmborough transport through the ages. (SF)

Park Square pre - 1911. (SF)

S. FARMER & Co., Piano Merchants

In 1921 Irving Berlin suggested we "Say It With Music". He was more than forty years late, for the Farmer family had been doing just that in Luton since 1880. The name of Farmer meant one thing in Luton - music of all kinds, radios, gramophones and records which then spun at 78

1910 from internal injuries received when hit by a drunken driver in a pony and trap! After a few years the Bute Street shop was closed, and Sydney, moving to Luton with his wife Jane, lived over their new shop at 2 Wellington Street, next to the Home & Colonial Tea Co. Moving home to 42 Stuart Street and then to 22 Studley Road, they had three children, Kathleen,

Left to right, Sydney Farmer, Norman Farmer, Derek Farmer. (DF)

revolutions per minute. Or you could do it yourself with pianos, fiddles and flutes straight off the shelf; a sousaphone might take a little longer!

Albert Farmer, from Biggleswade and believed to be a market gardener, founded the firm in a little place in Bute Street together with business partner Fred Gostelow who was the professional in the business, being for many years the organist at St. Mary's, Luton's Parish Church. Albert, who was then living in Bolton Road, later took in as a partner his cousin Sydney, son of Hannah and Francis who also lived in Biggleswade. Francis died in

Constance and Sydney Norman who was always known as Norman. In 1903 Kathleen married Leslie Merchant of the established house furnishing family in Manchester Street, and in 1925 Constance married Percy Congreve of the hat manufacturing family in Union Street. In 1918 Norman, who had been educated at Dunstable Grammar School, returned from war service in France, and married Mabel Blows. They first lived in Biscot Road, but later moved to Harpenden. It was he who was to continue the family business having spent some years in piano factories in London and final tuning experience in

The connecting premises through from George Street to Wellington Street. (DF)

Steinways being displayed; and also the Boudoir models which were intended for use in a ladies private bedroom. Costing 23 guineas cash, you could choose to pay 14/6d (72p) a month instead. Farmers were sole agents for the new £65 Pianola which could be played by hand or music roll, and also the Aeolian Orchestrelle which cost between £24 and £600. These offered unique devices to the owner which were the Metrostyle to assist in playing unfamiliar compositions, and the Thermolist to accent individual melody notes. In 1900 pianos were advertised on easy terms from 5/- (25p) per month, and organs at 10/6 (52½p) per month. Staff piano repairer, Walter Tilley,

Steinway Hall.

Around the corner No. 83 George Street, a larger unit, was added to the Wellington Street shop with the ability to walk through from one to the other, the family then leasing the corner buildings. Tobacconists Lewis of Westminster and a sweet shop were occupying these premises in between. Looting of stock and damage to the shop took place during the early hours of Sunday 20th July 1919 at the height of the riots following the peace celebrations when Luton Town Hall was burnt down. The shop, which was just across the road, had the plate glass windows broken and gramophones, a pianola and a grand piano pulled out onto the pavement. Farmers were one of the first dealerships to be appointed by Murphy Radio which was highly prized. They were also especially proud to hold the local agency for His Masters Voice, the horn gramophone complete with Nipper the dog often being displayed in the window. Pianos were a large part of the business for many years; Bechsteins, and

83 George Street following the riots of July 1919. (DF)

travelled daily to Luton from his London home. George Thunhurst was the staff French polisher and Charles Pearce and his son George were in charge of piano removals, using a sash window crane when required. Dorothy Glover looked after the record sales and in charge of the music department was Miss Lillian Winter who later taught piano on the upper floor studio, Elsie Toyer having done so earlier. Joan Sparvell, who later managed the music department, became Mayoress of Dunstable after her marriage. A number of local music teachers used the studio room, among them the violinist Leslie Dawson. Always known as "Uncle Tom", the shop manager for many years was Thomas Henry Catherall who was introduced to the firm by Fred Gostelow. He spent most of his working life with the Farmers, serving with three generations. He was an excellent tuner much sought after by concert artists, but displeasure was evident if he was asked to alter the pitch of their concert pianos! He repaired stringed instruments and some woodwind and reed organs, but his workshop did not tackle brass. However, wind-up gramophones came under him and later he introduced 'wireless'! During World War II, together with the ministry inspectors at the Vauxhall factory, he set up a testing and calibration facility for the No. 19 radio in the Churchill tank which enabled Farmers to keep an engineer in their service department. A team of outdoor piano tuners covered a wide area, but in town tuning was covered by Wilfred Fox. A 'mature' blind man, he was well-known in Luton, where his swinging white stick ensured he had a clear path along busy streets. He had an extensive knowledge of the town and could find any address.

From 1945, for more than 20 years, John Thompson was manager of both music and record departments. He was Chairman of the Luton Music Club, and in the Town Hall organised many public music evenings promoting Farmer's record and music sales. In 1962 these events moved into the new Library Theatre as part of the Luton Music Club programme. Farmers maintained a good relationship with local education authorities supplying a wide range of instruments, music, records and audio equipment, and pianos with the tuning service. Two large Bechstein grands and numerous upright pianos were kept for hire. Covering most major musical events, concert grands were hired from Steinway Hall if required. They also supported local concerts and record issues by Arthur Davies and The Luton Girls' Choir. During the war Norman turned to concert promoting, bringing a number of first class orchestras and artists to the Alma Theatre. A successful branch was opened in Dunstable, first at 3 West Street and later at 2 Church Street.

Sydney died in 1945 and Norman ten years later at the age of 62. At his funeral Rev. Fletcher recalled Norman's interest in the Methodist Church, Harpenden Photographic Society and the Harpenden Schools Festival, and said "He was a perfectionist, with him there was always one stage further to go". When he had completed his stint in the forces, Norman's son Derek at the age of 22 became the

The Connaught House shop in Upper George Street in 1961. (DF)

S. Farmer & Co. Ltd. moved into Day's larger premises, Connaught House, at 15-17 Upper George Street. Architect Clifford Shrimplin designed the new walk-around store, with a modern shop front fitted by W. H. Hudson of Chapel Street. Luton builders B. F. Parish carried through the alterations with H. F. Scriven from Bute Street in charge of electrics and Hillman & Co. of Cowper Street responsible for heating. The sparklingly modern premises offered two floors of everything musical, and now theatre bookings also. Do you remember Bush and Perdio radios, Fontana and Ace of Clubs records and maybe Dynatron television? They were all here.

Knowledge of their trade stood the Farmer family in good stead as the business prospered in size and repute, and now Farmers Music Centre was acknowledged for miles around, offering their vast experience and supplying anything from a gramophone needle to a grand piano. But in four years time, yet another irony! Derek sold the company back to David Robinson who retained the respected name of Farmer over the door and the undoubted abilities of Derek as a Director on the premises. However, eight months with a big retail group proved to Derek that he was a misfit. The feeling was

fourth generation to join the family firm. He had recently married Jean Dunn whom he had known since childhood. Derek's great interest was in the radio and television departments, but when his father died Derek became the sole proprietor and the many other matters of the business fell upon his young shoulders. His first move was to form a limited company.

During the 1950s, David Robinson of Robinson Rentals who owned the competitor Arthur Day in Upper George Street, approached Farmers on many occasions with offers to buy them out, but Derek always refused. Then in 1961, in an ironical move, the tables turned and Farmers bought Arthur Days from Robinson Rentals who had not been able to equal Farmers competition! This brought the Wellington Street and George Street properties onto the market as apparently mutual, so Derek was released from his contract and he was welcomed by one of his wholesale friends who was setting up an industrial electronics department. This job lasted for twelve years and was followed by ten years in electronic instrumentation. Derek Farmer finally retired to his Harpenden home where he lives to this day. Within five years Robinsons had sold again to Marshalls.

The Wellington Street and George Street shops are now Showboat and estate agents Connells. Insurance company Swinton occupies Connaught House.

One of Messrs. S. Farmer & Co's Piano and Organ Show Rooms, Wellington Street and George Street. (T.G. Hobbs)

Frank & Shirley's Ltd

Derived from the latin 'auctio', meaning an increase, an auction is a method of selling all kinds of property by which persons, in competition, make offers successively in advancing sums. So says the dictionary, and certainly for many years in Luton our subjects did just that, putting all kinds of property 'under the hammer'. Yet it had all progressed from enthusiasm gained at a Sunday morning boot sale!

Frank Horn was born in 1932 in Napier Road, Luton of Lutonian parents. They moved to Kingston Road and Frank attended Old Bedford Road School. His first job on leaving school was in the hardware department of the Luton Industrial Co-operative Society in New Bedford Road. Across the road in the Co-op Chemists shop worked Shirley Ginger, who had already been warned that the young boy in hardware tried to get to know all the new girls who joined the company. This was Frank, and Shirley was quite determined not to show any interest in him. However, he was very persistent and eventually they went to 'the pictures' together. Shirley was fifteen years old, and they never looked back. She also came from local families; her mother came from Markyate and her father from Slip End. Born in Runley Road in Luton in 1936, the family moved to Manor Road, Caddington when she was three months old.

In 1955 Frank and Shirley were married at High Town Methodist Church, and they both had jobs at Caddington Post Office. Three years later, the first of their many joint ventures commenced when they established a general store at 11 St. Augustines Avenue, Luton, living over the shop for the next eight years. Their family began to arrive, so in 1965 a move back to Caddington was made, living with Mum and Dad. Frank continued the greengrocery van delivery round which he had commenced from the shop, and for some years did house maintenance for Dunstable Borough Council. Shirley made hats at home for hat manufacturer Albert, and later became a forelady with Berman Hats.

One Sunday morning in 1968 they set up their table at a boot sale in the grounds of the Hertfordshire Moat House on the Watling Street near Dunstable, hoping to raise a little extra cash. They took just £13, but noticed that the lady with the next table was very busy selling brass collectables and taking very much more cash than they were. Frank, always confident, said "One day we'll take a thousand!". They were hooked and went buying at the auctions in Adelaide Street, Luton. Their purchases were sold on again at more boot sales, and also at Hemel Hempstead Wednesday market and Dunstable Friday market which Shirley did during her holiday breaks from the hat factory.

Their sales abilities were improving, and the next promotion, in 1973, was the organizing of antique fairs at Slip End village hall. Also, for the next two years and together with a friend, Shirley took a shop in John Street, Luton selling second-hand goods. Trio Products were

Auction House in Crescent Road, previously the Co-op Bakery.

next door, and in 1980 Frank and Shirley's first auction took place upstairs above their woodyard. When Trio moved to High Town, Frank and Shirley's first company came into being, as they took over the larger premises next door and became Luton Multi-Auctions. Inside it became a complex tangle of used items. There could be little attempt at display. Second-hand furniture balanced on top of each other, there were many rolls of carpet, china, watches, prams, rails of cheap cloths and sometimes a rocking horse. It was a fascinating maze of time-worn chattels. House clearance was important business, and professional polishes and wools for use on antique furniture were supplied to the wholesale trade. Antique and collectable fairs were organized, a

very successful one locally at Wing in Buckinghamshire.

In time it was not only the goods that were crumbling, but the John Street building also, and then the roof began to leak. Enquiries were made about the now disused and empty building in Crescent Road that was once the busy bakery division of the Co-operative Wholesale Society. In 1996 this building was rented, and a move made from the John Street site. Frank & Shirley's Ltd. was formed and a new successful auction house came into being, known better as Luton Antiques Centre and Crescent Auctions. Smaller units inside this huge structure were rented to local people who had antiques to sell, and general auctions took place every Thursday evening and monthly on Sundays. As auctioneer Frank often 'knocked down' as many as 350 lots in an evening to enthusiastic crowds bidding by waving their numbered paddles or by imperceptibly nodding to the auctioneer. The good fortunes of Frank and Shirley continued here for four years, finally surrendering to an unacceptable rent increase, and closing down in 2000. The building is now occupied by the Luton beer and wine wholesalers Barrel Booze Ltd.

Over a period of nine years, Frank and Shirley had six sons who were all at some time involved in the family business. Vernon, Nigel, and Clifford assisted at

Nigel Horn preparing lots prior to an auction. (SHo)

Shirley and Frank Horn pictured on the day they left Luton Auction Centre.

Crescent Road, Clifford taking over from his father as auctioneer. Darren is now working in Germany and Trevor has his own double-glazing business. Ashley, with his wife Leslie, and Nigel, with his wife Joanne have, since the closure of Crescent Road, reintroduced the monthly Sunday antique fairs and auction evenings in the Slip End village hall. Nigel also ships furniture to Spain for auction there. Although Frank & Shirley Ltd. is now history, retirement is not a word that they personally accept. Frank travels widely selling books at national antique fairs under the title Books for Collectors, and also personally collects Carnival glassware. Shirley runs the office for the book venture from their premises in Toddington, and also collects Luton memorabilia. They still live in the family home in Caddington that Shirley moved into 65 years ago and, of course, they enjoy their nine grandchildren.

VICTOR FURSE

The Briton Ferry sailed from Baglan near Port Talbot in Glamorgan across the Bristol Channel to Ilfracombe in Devon. William Furse was a marine engineer on the ferry and he and his wife Anne lived in nearby Neath, surrounded by collieries and engineering works. They had seven sons, the sixth being Victor William who was born in 1915.

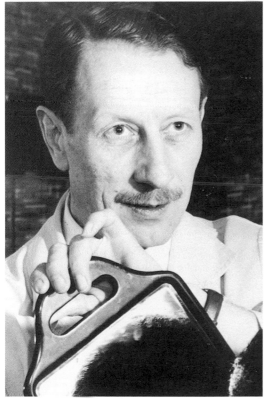

Victor Furse. (IF)

Victor attended the school which was next door to their home, but sadly when he was moving up to the Port Talbot Secondary School at the age of 11, his father died. His job for life began when he left school at 15 to become an apprentice hairdresser at a shop in Neath where first he learned to make the tea and sweep up the hair from the floor! At 21 he took 'digs' in Luton after successfully answering a national advertisement from Button Brothers who had a hairdressing department within their outfitting shop and which at that time was at 53 George Street on the corner with George Street West. One of Victor's duties was to cut the hair of patients in Luton's Bute Cottage Hospital and his attention was particularly drawn to one of the nurses resident there.

War interrupted this hoped-for liaison, with Victor serving first in the Beds & Herts Regiment and then as a Sergeant in the Royal Norfolk Regiment being in France shortly after D-Day. During this time the pretty nurse was learning midwifery in Birmingham and later in South Wales. However in 1944 at St. Catherine's Church in Baglan, Victor married his nurse Irene Burns, and as the War came to an end Irene continued domiciliary midwifery in Luton, while Victor returned to his old job with Buttons. During their first months of marriage Vic lodged in Lyndhurst Road, and Rene lived in the Midwive's Hostel in Napier Road, but they soon set up home in Cutenhoe Road and later in Graham Gardens.

In 1959 Victor was sufficiently confident with his tonsorial art to leave Buttons and open his own luxury gentlemen's hairdressing salon at 6 King Street, Luton which was previously the

6 King Street, approx 1960. (IF)

floor offered sales and service of electric shavers. Local advertisements suggested they had the lowest prices on Remington, Ronson, Philips, Kobler, Sunbeam and Schick shavers. One evening Victor held a public contest in the foyer of the Savoy Cinema when men were invited to see how long it would take to remove a fully-grown beard with a new Remington electric shaver. His salon was one of the premier gent's hairdressers in the town centre for 21 years, and during this time a second branch was opened in Vernon Place, Dunstable. In 1980, when the adjoining Midland Bank which owned the premises required to extend and use 6 King Street, Vic withdrew from hairdressing and moved into a smaller unit at 19 George Street, where for three more years he sold and serviced electric shavers. Bryan Walduck, one of the King Street staff, purchased the goodwill and, in George Street, continues to give the same efficient service.

home of the Co-Operative Permanent Building Society. The first floor salon had four chairs, always with Victor in attendance at one of them, and the ground

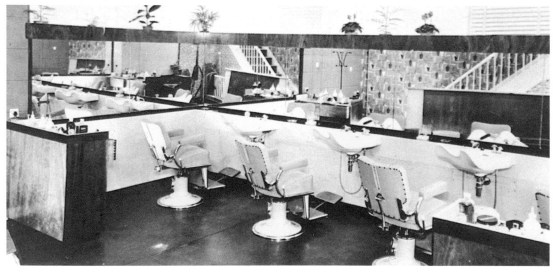

The first floor gents hairdressing sdalon. (IF)

Vic producing a "Viva" in retiremnet.

interest in fly fishing became paramount. His enthusiasm was partly responsible for the forming of the North Norfolk branch of The Fly Dressers Guild, and at the age of 80 he became one of East Anglia's leading fly dressers. In this interest he remembered his connections with Luton and named all the new flies he made after various Vauxhall motorcars. The 'Viva', a new design of fly which he devised, became internationally one of the most successful in resevoir fishing and holds the national record for catching brown trout. Vic also had a love of practical jokes, and was known to family and friends as a 'prankster'.

Rene had her own successful career in nursing, eventually becoming Nursing Officer for the Borough of Luton. She was responsible for District Nursing, Health Visiting and Midwifery in the town for 13 years between 1961 and 1974.

Retirement came in 1983 with a move to North Walsham where Vic's lifelong

Victor died in 1996 at the age of 81, and Rene died in 1999 aged 82. Their daughter and son and their families of 8 children all live in a village on the outskirts of Luton.

GREENERS

Remember when claret was 14/- (70p) a dozen bottles, and whisky sold for 36/- (£1.80) a dozen? I doubt it, but Lawrence Greener did! He started in the wine trade in the order department of a wine merchant in Pall Mall, London in 1914 at the age of thirteen.

He came to Luton, with his new wife, as manager of R. H. Marks, wine and spirit merchants, in George Street. This now forms part of the British Home Stores buildings. When Mr. Marks died, his widow decided to close

Lawrence Greener. (DS)

the business and sell the property, which then became the fashion shop Paris House. It was Lawrence Greener's ambition to start his own business, so in 1938 he opened at 60 Wellington Street on the corner with Stuart Street. Despite the war starting so soon afterwards, it was a great success. The general public began to go in for dinner wines but because very few houses had suitable cellars, the average customer used the merchant's shop as his storage. Lawrence and his wife had three daughters, living first in Wardown Crescent, naming their house 'Petitor', remembering the seaside resort where they spent their honeymoon, and later in Carlton Crescent.

After the war, holidaymaking and travelling abroad increased many people's interest in wine and Mr. Greener had definite views regarding vintages. He said "You have vintages on this and vintages on that, but a good merchant will never sell a wine, whatever its vintage, if it's not a good one". He was also disappointed at the falling off in demand for port, pointing out that Britain was the only country to guarantee the name of this fine wine.

When the new Stuart Street dual-carriageway was proposed, his shop together with several others in Wellington Street, and all of one side of Stuart Street, was purchased under a compulsory order and eventually demolished. Greeners, one of the few family businesses in the local wine and spirit field, made the necessary

Wine merchants, R.H. Marks in George Street. (RJo)

Greeners wine store at 60 Wellington Street. (DS)

move to new premises in October 1965. The shoe shop vacated by W. Mooring & Son at 45 Wellington Street was enlarged and modernised, it also having the advantage of a fine cellar.

As at the previous shop, the day-to-day running of the new business was supervised by Mr. Greener's son-in-law Barry le Boutillier. He had joined the firm in 1950, quickly gaining valuable experience in the trade. In 1965 he was the guest of Monsieur and Madam Claude Taittinger at their chateau at Rheims in the champagne district of France, where he was taken on a tour of their five miles of cellars. Mrs. Rita Bell was another familiar figure behind the counter of Greeners for many years.

In the 1960s, with pricing controls removed and supermarkets beginning to appear, it became necessary to move with the times. In November 1967 traditional counter service and free delivery was abandoned and Greeners became the first cash and carry wine outlet in Luton with prices greatly reduced. Late evening trading was usual, and in addition two hours opening over the Sunday lunchtime was introduced. This proved an overwhelming success, this style of business continuing until Barry le Boutillier retired, when the business was closed and the premises sold in 1986. This building is now the tandoori restaurant Shapla. Lawrence Greener died in 1975.

HARMANS

House Furnishers, Jewellers, Outfitters

The three golden balls, the once familiar pawnbrokers sign, hung high up on the second floor of 92/94 Park Street for 83 years. By charging a modest interest, 'Uncle' provided an essential service; suits, sheets, blankets and jewellery would be 'popped' especially on Mondays - rent day - and probably redeemed the next week or following pay day. If the borrower did not redeem the article in 12 months, the pawnbroker could put the goods into his sale stock, but anything over a £1 had to go to auction. The sign came from the coat of arms of the Medici family and was introduced to London from Italy in medieval times by Lombard, the bankers and moneylenders. The popular explanation for the positioning of the balls was that there were two chances to one that what was pawned would be redeemed. The pawnbroking premises in Park Street were named Lombard House.

George Edward Harman was born in 1853, the son of Henry who was the licensed victualler of The Swan Inn at Denham in Buckinghamshire. George worked first for Mr. J. Butcher, a pawnbroker in Uxbridge and later in his shop in Bute Street, Luton where he met, and in 1878, married Amelia "Minnie" Shoosmith. Minnie was the daughter of Frederick Shoosmsith, a shoe-maker in

Left to right, George Harman, Henry Harman, Philip Harman. (PH)

Hastings Street. Work experience was gained in Exeter, London and Southampton before they set up home at 96 Park Street in 1884. Minnie and George had four sons, only Henry George, born in 1881, living to a good age; his brother, Frederick Howard, who had worked at the Watford branch, being killed at Ypres, aged 34, in 1917.

Business progressed well, for two years

The 1920s Park Street premises of Harman & Shoosmith. (PH)

compulsory purchase order in 1972, this is now the only building of the original business which survives.

Minnie Harman's brother Frederick had assisted with finance over the years, whilst he held a post in Tsarist Russia, the name of Harman & Shoosmith appearing over the shops, but in 1930 Frederick was bought out and the title of Harman & Son became known. Henry George, the son who had served his pawnbroking apprenticeship in Limehouse, became the prime mover in the business. He had married Kate Pedley, daughter of F.J. Pedley, signwriter and gilder, of 52 Cheapside, Luton, and their second son Philip was born in 1923. Success continued for many years due not only to hard work and long hours, but also to the influx of people into the town and the enlargement of the Park Town area for working class people with whom they mainly traded. Also the arrival of the Vauxhall Motors factory had put the Harman shops on the route for workers who lived across the fast-growing town. It is recalled that furniture manager Albert Hoare would watch for competitor Charles Farmbrough taking a walk along Park Street on the opposite side of the road, then crossing to walk casually past Harmans in order to note their furniture prices. He didn't know that he had been seen and that showcards had been quickly changed in the window displays to deceive him. These were restored to their original

later cottages on adjoining land were demolished and tall elegant new premises built to house the expanding trade. In 1904 they advertised "the great want of the period is to know how to spend money to the best advantage", presumably they would show you. Nos. 94-92 sold men's clothing and tools, whilst the taking of pledges was conducted via a passage to the rear of the premises. Nos. 90-88 sold furniture and household goods and No. 86, previously a general shop, was converted to a jewellers in 1920. The interior of No. 86 was beautifully fitted out in red mahogany, with curved plate glass windows at the entrance, supplied by T. & E. Neville, the local joiners and undertakers.   School Walk, which led to Queen Square School, separated these shops from the next acquisition which was No. 84, previously the S. J. Bourne hat factory, which in 1935 was rebuilt by H.C. Janes to become a further furniture showroom on three floors. Following the

prices once he had passed.

Prices at Harmans were always competitive as a sales brochure for 1933 shows. Men's flannel trousers from 3/11d (20p), boys shirts from 1/- (5p), large towels 6d (2.5p) each; heavy oak dining chairs from 8/11d (45p), strong full sized cots on rubber tyred castors cost 14/6d (73p), 22ct. gold wedding rings from

shop over in 1929 and when they vacated it in 1984 to move into the Arndale Centre, a medieval frame was revealed which now forms part of the Stockwood Craft Museum building.

A further branch in Queens Road, Watford had been opened in 1905, and remained until 1978. G.E. Harman who was then living in Stockwood Crescent,

84-96 Park Street, Luton. (PH)

12/6d (63p), or in 9ct. from 5/- (25p); lawn mowers from 16/6d (83p), and "plimsolls made in Great Britain of British materials by British workers" cost 8³/₄d (4p) each child's pair. Harmans offered a club in which you could "have what you like, pay what you like, when you like", and they added a shilling to every £1 you paid in. Around 1920 a china shop at 12 Park Square, was opened bringing Harmans closer to the town centre, and offering "a special show of vases, tea, dinner and toilet ware". Halfords took this

died in 1931 aged 77. He had served as a Liberal Town Councillor for six years and was also President of the East Ward Liberal Association. He was a founder member of the Luton & Dunstable Tradesmen's Association, being Treasurer for 19 years and also Deacon and a Trustee of the Union Chapel in Castle Street.

Harman & Son continued, with young Philip joining his father in the business in 1939 at the age of 16, having attended Luton Modern School in both the old and new buildings. In 1949 he married

Margaret Chandler. In 1960 Henry George (Harry) and Philip formed a new partnership, G. Harman (Luton) Ltd., but five years later Harry, who had been a Luton Rotarian, died aged 84. Philip's real love in the business had always been the jewellery, watch and clock departments, recalling buying scrap silver when it was valued at only 2/6d (12½p) a troy ounce. He remembers, with a smile, how dustmen would look for silver items in collected household rubbish and bring them in to sell, he eventually instructing them how to look for hallmarks! WWII intervened and one by one staff were called to join the Forces until finally only Philip, Harry and one faithful porter remained as the sirens began to sound. The German landmine explosion on Sunday night 30th September 1940 over the Corporation bus garage in Park Street shattered every window in the vicinity and 84-94 was no exception. Shovelling broken glass through an open first floor window into the street

below on the morning after is one memory recalled by Philip. Large sheets of plate glass being then unobtainable, the display windows were boarded up apart from central 'peepholes' and remained so until after VE and VJ days had been celebrated. The pledge shop closed in 1963 and compulsory purchase ended the life of 86-94 Park Street in 1972 when the bridge was built carrying the Park Viaduct section of the inner-ring road over Park Street. Dorsett Business Machines moved into No.84 on which the Harman name is still just visible on the tiled facade. It is now used by Series-3 Marketing.

So ended the business venture of George, Henry and Philip Harman who served the local community for almost 90 years through three generations. Philip and his wife Margaret now enjoy retirement in Luton, regularly attending meetings of the Friends of Luton Museum where Philip serves as a committee member, and was also magazine editor for many years.

G. R. H. HAY

Previously Luton's Central Cafe owned by the Primett family who lived next door at No.20 Cheapside, No's 22 and 24 became, in 1960, the premises of dispensing chemists G.R.H. Hay Ltd. Upstairs remained a restaurant using the name The Kan-Wong which was managed by K. Man and Y. Wong.

22-24 Cheapside, Luton in 1960. (MHa)

George Robert Henderson Hay, who preferred to be known as Bob, was one of eight children born into a farming family in Banff in the north-east of Scotland. His life interest in pharmacy began as a junior in the chemist's shop in his home town, going on to qualify as a pharmacist and gaining a bronze medal as outstanding student at the Herriot Watt University in Edinburgh. Boots the progressive cash chemists of the day attracted him, becoming manager of their branch on the quayside at Oban, and later at Stamford in Lincolnshire. Acting as relief manager at Boots in Chesterfield one day brought him his future bride, when he met assistant Mary Knott who was busy dressing the windows. They married in 1944.

Wartime duties found him as a sergeant-major in the Royal Army Medical Corps, returning in peacetime to Gregory's, the chemists at Mildenhall in Suffolk, where he lived with his wife and family above the shop. It was from here that he successfully answered an advertisement for a job in Luton. Ron Hopkins engaged him as manager of the Hitchin Road, Stopsley branch of R. A. Hopkins Ltd, with whom he stayed for the next eight years, leaving to open his own shop in Luton's Cheapside in 1960.

It was a very successful chemist's shop run by Mary and Bob and six extra staff, where they dispensed hundreds of "scripts" every week (prescriptions to you and me!). Throughout a pharmacist's career he is answerable to The Pharmaceutical Society of Great Britain, and Bob Hay's conduct, knowledge and dedication to his profession more than fulfilled their standards. Everyone was able to call on him at times of medical crisis and his female customers in particular knew that a word in his ear regarding their personal problems would be dealt with quietly and efficiently, very often saving a visit to the doctor. In 1966 a fire in the

Bob and Mary Hay were always ready to serve. (MHa)

restaurant above the shop devastated their business. Water damage necessitated taking it across the road into a vacant shop for almost a year whilst their own was rebuilt and refitted. During this time Bob was Secretary of both the Bedfordshire Pharmaceutical Society and also of St. Ninian's Church in Villa Road, Luton. He was also elected President of the Luton, Dunstable and District Chamber of Trade.

Bob sadly had to close his shop in 1972, only when forced to do so by the coming of the Arndale Centre, but went on to assist in three Luton pharmacies, the Co-op in New Bedford Road, Morgan's in Dunstable Road and Sampson's in High Town Road, finally retiring aged 78 when Sampson's was sold. Bob died in 1996, aged 85. I was proud to know him as a good friend for half of those years. Mary still lives in Luton with a daughter, a son and three grandsons around her.

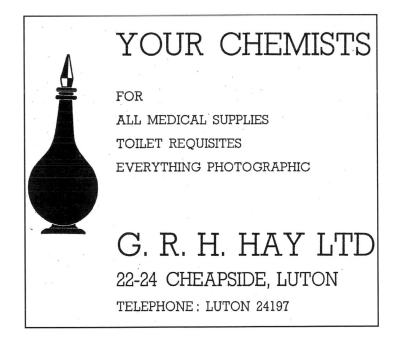

Hickman & Son (Luton) Ltd
MAKERS OF THE "PETER PAN LOAF"

Before the First World War every village in the county had its own baker. In Luton and Dunstable there were a staggering 60, and within three-quarters of a mile of Luton's Chapel Street there were eight bakehouses. Yet this is where, after

Ken Hickman (left) and Harry Hickman. (BMc)

the end of the First World War for which he had lied about his age to join, and a complete stranger to the town, Ernest William Kenneth Hickman bought a shop and bakery at No. 19, on the corner with Victoria Street, previously occupied by Arthur Hill. The young man from small beginnings in Oxfordshire was to become a big baker in Luton.

He was born in 1897 to Charlotte and William Henry in the little village of Bessels Leigh, but later moving to Wolverton. It was in 1919 that, with his baker father, he formed W. H. Hickman & Son. The weekly production was 1600 loaves which were delivered by horse and

cart. (By the mid 1970s this number of loaves was produced in an hour). His original inclination was to be a pianist, and in the days of silent films he had played the accompaniment to the comedies and tragedies on the screen in a village cinema in Buckinghamshire. However, it was not unnatural that he should feel the pull of the trade and eventually planned his future in the direction of bread and confectionery.

Business progressed well, but in 1929 William Henry died, and one year later Ernest entered into a partnership with his brother Albert who was fourteen years his junior. The capital of the firm consisted of £326 and the partners agreed that "EWKH would draw a sum not exceeding £3 a week, and AHH a sum not exceeding £2 a week". In 1934 Articles of Association were drawn up for Hickman & Son (Luton) Ltd., with a share capital of £1000. It will be simpler if we now refer to the directors in the way that they were always known, Ernest was always Ken and Albert was always Harry. Ken had married Ada Ireland at the Ceylon Baptist Church. They met when Ken was making bread deliveries at her father's corner grocery shop in Grove Road. They lived in Kennington Road, moving later to Marlborough Road, and had two daughters, Betty and Marjorie. Harry had married Zena Stonebridge in Luton, lived in Sherwood Road, and also had two daughters, Janet and Susan. Within two

Ken Hickman (centre) with the Luton Association of Master Bakers float in the 1935 Silver Jubilee procession. (C.R. Crawley)

years a purpose-built bakery in Sherwood Road was opened, and used for bread production. The basement of 19 Chapel Street now being used for cakes only always produced a splendid smell, and if you looked down through the grating windows you could watch the girls putting the cherries on the cakes. Further necessary expansion came in 1952 with the opening of the Wingate Road bakery, "a specially built modern bakery which eventually attained one of the highest positions in the trade in Bedfordshire". It was a major outlay for the brothers, also spending their last £200 purchasing a bread slicing machine. The plant bakery produced crusty or sliced and wrapped loaves called "The Peter Pan Loaf...it never grows old!", a phrase Ken was always proud of. By this time there was a shop at 96 High Town Road, as well as at 19 Chapel Street, and bread was 'trucked' to businesses all over the country.

The beginning of the national decline of the independent family baker began with the Bill which banned continuous night-time baking in underground premises, and was the writing on the wall for Luton's 13 underground bakeries. In 1939 there were still 30 bakers in Luton but the wartime subsidy system penalised the small man. During the war, from 1941 to 1944, the Hickman brothers ran bakery classes in the Luton Technical College in Park Square. In the mid 1950s the big millers like Ranks and Spillers moved into

Advert.

the bread retailing line by buying out many of the independent bakers who had been ignoring their products in favour of cheaper imported flour. In addition the building of the M1 motorway saw our local counties more easily served by the larger London and Birmingham based bakeries. Statistics show that in 1945 there were 9,500 members of the National Association of Master Bakers and by 1974 there were only 3,800.

In 1957 the two brothers sold out to the Spillers French group. Ken retired, but Harry continued with the new owners in the position of Group Production Manager. "O, do you know the Muffin Man?"...well of course you do, for in the mid 1970's it was Harry Hickman! He had a soft spot

for the muffins that were made to an old family recipe, and made 70 dozen an hour. Then he purchased a muffin machine from America and had it installed in Wingate Road, the only one of its kind in the country at that time. The new griddle produced 6,000 muffins an hour, which were sold under the Spillers brand, and also to Sainsburys and Marks & Spencer. Sometimes the muffins would not come out of the tins, but Harry solved this by rolling them in a Quaker meal. On one occasion when there was a problem with the supplier of bridge rolls for the Queen's garden party, Hickmans were asked to make them to the Palace's recipe and despatch them by taxi to Buckingham Palace.

On August 14th 1976, Spillers French made the surprise decision to close the Luton plant, making 200 staff redundant, thus bringing to an end 57 years of this old established bakery. Spillers French were being strangled by the extra discounts being demanded by supermarkets to the point where they were only making a few pence on each loaf and on some lines no profit at all. Harry, who loved the baking industry, remained until he had helped everyone find another job. He always regretted the sell-out to Spillers and viewed the closure with great sadness. The bakery and shop in Chapel Street had already gone with the building of the Chapel Viaduct.

In the field of voluntary work, Ken Hickman excelled. He became a councillor in 1942 and Mayor of Luton in May 1955. He recalled in his inaugural speech that he remembered as a young man standing in

Putting dough into individual muffin tins in the Wingate Road bakery in 1955. (BMc)

George Street and watching the Town Hall burn, and wondered what sort of town he had selected in which to work and live. He was also President of the Master Baker's Association, President of the Luton Chamber of Trade during the second world war, President of Luton Rotary Club, President of the Luton Band, Vice-President of Luton Swimming Club and a Freemason. With his wife they founded the Park Street Old Peoples Club. When he was awarded the O.B.E. in 1961 for political and public services, the "Luton News" leader was headed "Modest Honour, Modest Man". He was a little superstitious after a horse he had bought

on a Sunday became lame, and after that never again wrote a cheque on a Sunday! In retirement he enjoyed his holiday flat in Bournemouth, and died in 1974. Harry, also a freemason, spent his retirement at his Bedfordshire home, Yellow Farm at Tilsworth. Disaster struck this 500 years old listed building when a lorry touched an overhead cable and caused a fire in the thatched roof. It was during the firemen's strike and the house was totally destroyed, but later rebuilt. Harry died in 1992.

Harry's daughter Janet, now living in Goring-by-Sea, still has the Chain of Office of the Luton Master Baker's Association bearing the names of both Ken and Harry and also bakery manager John Desborough. She also holds their historic Minute Book which, in 1918, records reluctant discussion of using a potato mash in the bread. Decisions are also noted concerning joining the local Tradesmen's Association, mentioning Mr. Bloomfield and Mr. Rudd, both well-remembered names in local baking.

They always met in local restaurants; The George in George Street, The Central in Cheapside and The Thrift in Stuart Street. Ken's daughter Betty still lives in Luton. Both Ken and Harry Hickman served our town well and besides earning our respect, it could be said that they earned an honest crust!

CHARLIE & MONTY INGLIS

Recalling the time when barber-surgeons also practiced blood-letting, the famous red and white barber's pole extended out from the premises at 68 Park Street, Luton. There, next to the narrow alleyway which was known as Park Place and which led up to Ball Court, the Inglis family shaved and trimmed for more than seventy years.

Charles Inglis went into the same trade as his father who worked for a barber in London's Strand. Charles married twice and had two daughters, Dora and Lillian, and one son Montague who was born in 1905. The family at first lived a few doors away from the Cock Inn, at 42 Park Street, then above their barber's shop, but later moved to Harcourt Street which enabled them to extend the salon at No. 68 back into what had been the family kitchen. At one time Charles Junior was cutting hair at 42 whilst his father was doing the same at 68. Dora could recall how her father insisted when she was 14 years old that she should help in the salon on Saturday mornings. Her job, which she hated, was to lather the rough chins of the farm labourers who had come in for their weekly shave, but for some it was their monthly shave! She was also given 1/6 (7½p) to scrub the floor at the end of the day, which was 8 p.m. In order to catch the men on the Vauxhall early shift, morning opening was 6 a.m. when the stand outside the shop would fill with bicycles. There were four chairs and sometimes it was so busy that customers were given a cloakroom ticket on entry so that they were dealt with in order. In the 1930s, a haircut cost 6d. (2½p). Dora's husband, Wally Upton, who was an engineering lecturer, and is now 94 years old, remembers modifying one of the chairs so that it could rotate on its base. Charlie's son Monty joined the business straight from school, taking over when his father retired, and remaining until his own retirement. One assignment away from the salon was to visit both the Bute Hospital and the Workhouse in Dunstable Road to haircut and shave the patients, occasionally also being asked to assist with removals to the mortuary!

Both Charlie and Monty were keen sportsmen. Charlie trained enthusiasts who planned to swim the English Channel, and also helped train local man George Webber to gain a silver medal in an athletics event during the 1924 Olympics held in Paris. He could often be seen running around the Osborne Road area, known then as the Marslips. Monty was a gold medal cyclist with the Luton Wheelers, and it was here that he met his future wife Leila whom he married after an 18 years courtship. They were active in the Christian Science Society.

During WWII, assistants Reg and Bert were called away, but Monty was unfit for active service. His wife Leila had to quickly learn the job and believed she was at that time the only woman cutting men's hair. In 1975, assistant Bert purchased the business when Leila and Monty retired to a bungalow in Lynwood Avenue, Luton where Monty died in 1991. By 1976 the haircutting had stopped, and No.68 Park Street is now the premises of Perfect Pizza.

The salon in 1950. Left to right, Reg Shepherd, Bert, Leila Inglis and Monty Inglis. (HW)

KAMERA-MEX

This is the story of a man who progressed from his one-man business in Adelaide Street, Luton to an important position within the Disney Studios in Los Angeles. Locally he may not be remembered by everyone, but for those who knew him he remains treasured in their memory.

Ellis Smith at his Adelaide Street workbench in 1956.

Ellis Smith, often known as Mick, was born in 1924 in Bermondsey, on the south bank of the Thames. His father was wounded in World War I, and died when Ellis was only four months old, his childhood memories being only of moving house many times, including once to Croydon into a home for wounded veterans' children. A later move was to Markyate, and then when 11 years old to Luton, attending Surrey Street School.

At the age of 14 he went into the drawing office of George Kent Ltd. and during WW2 into their Admiralty Research Dept, training to be an instrument maker. This was a reserved occupation but he eventually joined the RAF serving in Belgium, France and Germany. His mother, who was running a boarding house in Stockwood Crescent, at one time looked after 20 evacuees from London.

After the war Ellis worked as a technician for Cecil Kershaw & Sons, the Leeds camera manufacturers, and then homesick for Luton searched the columns of "The Luton News" for a chance to return home. He obtained a position with Peeling & Komlosy in Victoria Street, Dunstable, who were the Zeiss camera importers at that time. With wife Kathleen, whom he had met in the RAF, he lived in The Pyghtle on Farley Hill Estate. Very soon the decision was taken to have a trial year as a camera mechanic on his own, and so in a rented disused hat factory in Bury Park Road Kamera-Mex was born. Times were hard, for despite visiting camera shops, chemists and professional photographers over a wide area twice a week, little business came his way. In fact his first real job after ten months was from chemists Timothy White and Taylor, who provided work which was charged out to them at two shillings (10p) and then had to be invoiced. This was done, and even a discount offered if paid promptly, but it

Ellis Smith (left) and the author (right) visiting a London Photo-Fair in 1957.

was never paid, the only bad debt encountered in all his working life!

In 1955 he moved into premises at 18a Adelaide Street, long since vanished into the Luton Police Headquarters complex. Business improved, some work coming from RAF-Chicksands, and University Cameras gave him twenty camera repairs for a start and eventually all their work. They were later to offer him work from all their branches, but by now a word had surfaced which was to accurately describe the rest of his life. That word was 'wanderlust', for he had decided to emigrate. In 1958 the family set up home in Los Angeles, but Ellis had difficulty in finding work because any employee had to have been an American citizen for five years. Ellis never took American citizenship, remaining all his life proud to say he was British. He did later succeed in gaining work however, servicing Mitchell aerial cameras in San Fernando, and then with Zeiss in Pasadena. By now "life was

fabulous" with a big house, two cars and automatic annual pay increases. But it got better in 1963 when the Beaulieu Corporation asked him to set up their American franchises and repair shop. Then it got even better when he conceived his own ENS Camera Service and gained a contract to service the cameras in use at Universal Studios. He had it made and never looked back, working for Universal, Warner Brothers, Disney Studios and personal work for the stars, remembering especially Red Skelton, an enthusiastic photographer for whom he did a lot of work. But yet again that old wanderlust stepped in, and in 1978 he sold everything, business and home, and bought a personalised thirty-feet long recreation trailer and tow vehicle. The next period of their lives was spent travelling all over the United States, Canada and Mexico, staying in an amazing 575 different locations.

Ellis worked in England for twenty years, worked in the U.S.A. for twenty years and travelled throughout North America for twenty years. With their two sons and four grandchildren living in California, Kathleen and Ellis finally settled in Otis, Oregon. Each November they would travel down the coast into the warmer climes of southern California or Arizona and become what the people in the North called "snowbirds". Ellis became a victim of cancer in 1998 and died the following year. Shortly before he died he told me without hesitation, "I've had a wonderful life".

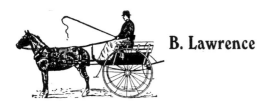

B. Lawrence

Bert Lawrence was born in Luton in 1886, the second son of nine children, six boys and three girls, born to Anne and Frederick. His father died very young leaving Anne to bring up a large family.

horses intended for work in the army, grazing and training them in a paddock on a part of Farley Hill which is now Whitehill Avenue; he had ponies and traps which he let out on hire and also wagonettes for Sunday School outings and he still continued with the fruit and vegetable barrow, to which he later added confectionery. In 1900, trading as A. Lawrence, his mother opened their first fruit and vegetable shop at 1 Tennyson

c1900 Bert Lawrence on his delivery cart outside the first shop at 1 Tennyson Road. His mother Anne is in the doorway. (WL)

When he was 12, he and his elder brother Amos began work, helping to keep the family intact. He used a hand barrow to sell fruit and vegetables, and as a young man followed many interests. He had a coal business; he was expert at breaking-in

Road on the corner with Baker Street. Before the first world war they moved the short distance to 59 Ashton Road on the corner with Cowper Street, changing the trading name to B. Lawrence. This was previously the premises of butchers T.H.

Durrant where large meat hooks still remain in the ceiling and the poultry hanging bar and gas lamps are still visible on the outside. Here the Lawrence business remained for almost a century, with coloured tiles in the wall either side of the entrance door depicting the quality produce on sale inside.

The two youngest sons had died in the great war, but Bert married Ellen Hull, whose father was a shepherd in Sundon and they set up home at 27 Cowper Street where they had three sons. Leslie

Alfred and Jane Lawrence (centre) pose with Geest representatives as winners of the national competition for the best display of Geest bananas in 1974. (WL)

In 1928, Walter Lawrence stands with his dog Prince outside the shop at 59 Ashton Road, (WL)

continued the interest in coal, working for his father selling coal purchased from Facer's; Walter worked with local laundry engineers Brown & Green based in Chaul End Lane and travelling the world as their sales director and Alfred joined his father in the fruit and vegetable business. Over the years he tried hard to retain the original atmosphere changing as little as possible in the shop, using an old-fashioned till and antiquated scales until 1995, when an electronic balance was introduced. Stan Parsons, who lived in Oxford Road, travelled daily to London's Covent Garden buying fruit for the shop, and fresh vegetables were delivered every day from market gardeners in Clophill. At one time trade was so good that a horse and cart was used to sell produce around the streets as late as 11p.m. and although there were four assistants in the shop, queues quite often formed. Walter recalls that Harold Hart, owner of the Markyate company Richmond Electronics, was a regular customer, always buying crates of fruit on each call, and often bringing his own valued customers from overseas with him.

Leslie died in 1997, and Alfred, after a period of ill health, died a year later.

Walter is still in Luton, happy in his retirement. After 96 years the shop closed down. Alfred's wife Jane, who still lives in Tennyson Road where her garden has won the Luton In Bloom competition, said that old people around there would miss it, that the shop was part of the community and that people came in with their problems and their gossip. When they closed one customer said with sadness, "I'll come in and cry on your shoulder".

The Greeks and the Romans enjoyed coursing, and King Henry VIII was known to place wagers in this sport. However, the residents of Luton would not have had the excitement of racing that most ancient breed, the greyhound, at Luton Stadium had it not been for a broken promise.

Alfred Walter Saunders, born in London in 1885, was a shoemaker. The day after he married Florence Fox they emigrated to Canada, where he opened a shoe shop in Toronto deciding that he could earn a better living by selling shoes than by making them. Their first son, Cyril, was born there in 1907 but Florence was homesick and they returned to England. At the outbreak of war in 1914, however, they returned to Canada where a second son, Norman, was born. Alfred had hoped to join the active Canadian forces, but he failed his medical and with his knowledge of footwear was given a job examining supplies of army boots. A second time they returned to England and to Golders Green, London at the end of hostilities, when Alfred gained a position as a commercial traveller with the company known as Dr. Scholls Foot Comforts. His area, however, was the whole of Scotland and it had to be covered using public transport.

A further change of direction was made in 1926 when Alfred and his family decided not to remain in Scotland. He came to Luton and took over as the proprietor of The Panama public house at 34 Waller Street, and the family lived above it. Barclay-Perkins were the supplying brewers at that time. Being next

Alfred Saunders outside his shop in Toronto, c1900. (NS)

to the covered market and public baths and opposite to the Grand Theatre, it was very busy indeed. Patrons at the theatre were invited in their programmes to cross the road and take tea in the Panama Lounge. During his time there Alfred was approached by a group who planned to open a dog-racing track on open ground near the road towards Bedford, (near what is now the Icknield Way roundabout), and offered him a share in this proposal. He was enthusiastic about this but on enquiring at a later date was told that agreements had all been completed and he was too late to take part. He was very displeased at being excluded, and decided there and then to counter this rejection by opening his own track. A site at Caddington was considered, but in 1931 a large field in Luton was purchased, and the Luton & Dunstable Greyhound Racing Club Ltd. opened, later to be renamed

Left to right, Cyril Saunders, Alfred Saunders, Norman Saunders plan the days racing in the stadium office in 1955. (NS)

Luton Stadium Ltd. There were five share-holders including a local bookmaker and a local farmer. The field adjacent to Skimpot Road stretched back almost to the railway line and twenty acres adjoining Dunstable Road were sold for housing.

It was an immediate success; track lighting was installed and racing at first took place on one weekday evening and twice on a Sunday until an Act of Parliament prevented Sunday racing. Later, meetings were to be at 7.30p.m. on Monday, Wednesday and Friday evenings.

Special buses were run from Williamson Street (now under St. Georges Square). Alfred and son Cyril were kept busy overseeing this whilst still also managing The Panama. Norman was at this time training to be a chef at London's Kensington Palace Hotel, but was soon needed to join his father and brother in their new venture. Both enterprises continued until 1942 when during World War II Cyril was a wireless telegraphist and Norman was a sergeant cook, both in the R.A.F. Alfred then concentrated on the dog-track, but in wartime racing only took place on Saturday afternoons as it was considered a detraction from the war effort, and of course lighting could not be used. In peacetime all the family were reunited, Cyril having married Maisie Unwin, lived in Villa Road and later in Studley Road; Norman had married Mary Berry, a Wren cook he had met in Sheerness during the war, and they set up home in Wychwood Avenue moving later to Old Bedford Road.

Luton Stadium now boasted an oval sand track of 405yds circumference with sprinkler watering system, and six dogs in each race chasing an inside Sumner hare. Amenities included a snack bar and light refreshments. Management had up to 150 dogs to choose from for each programme, and a trial day was held on alternate

Stewards exercise the dogs before a race. (NS)

Thursdays. Principal events were the Bedfordshire Derby held in May or June and the Bedfordshire St. Leger held in September. A Union Forecast Totalisator with eleven ticket selling machines had been installed in 1935, and in the early 1960's, high up in the roof of the main stand, a photofinish camera. For a period the author operated this camera, and the photofinish picture on the next page was taken at that time. In 1968 admission was 3/6 (17½p) and 4/6 (22½p) including race card and form details, and 1/- (5p) to park your car. There were often twenty book-makers in attendance, a staff of 45 and the public could reach 2,000. The racing card, in addition to being printed in all local newspapers, also appeared in the London Evening News and Evening Standard. The competitor's racing track on the Bedford Road survived only until 1934, when it was bought out by Luton Stadium Ltd, before being used for housing by builders Charles Jeyes.

In 1972, Arbiter Weston & Co, who controlled the ten-pin bowling alley in Stopsley, approached the stadium shareholders who rented to them part of their land on which they planned to build a similar bowling alley. A much larger entertainment centre and nightclub was eventually built which became known as Cesar's Palace. Arbiter Weston & Co. were later taken over by Ladbrokes who, for £500,000, purchased the stadium land with intention to build the current Skimpot Industrial Estate. Alfred Saunders had died in 1961, and Cyril died in 1985. Norman, now aged 86, still enjoys retirement with Mary in Luton.

The closure of the racing track caused concern and forty people demonstrated outside Luton Town Hall trying to persuade councillors to take up an offer from The Greyhound Owners Association to reopen the track, as opposed to that from Ladbrokes. The Luton Stadium held its last greyhound race and closed down in

October 1973. "The Luton News" reported that "A crowd of 500 overcoated and huddled together under their scarves and flat caps watched despondently the preparations for the last race. Shivering greyhounds were muzzled and bustled into their traps as the electric hare was cranked up to start for the last time." At the time of the closure there were about 200 greyhound owners in Luton with about 500 dogs. For 42 years the Luton Greyhound Stadium had provided cheap entertainment, at that time well-suited to their clientele.

A photofinish picture was required for this race on 6th May 1967.

McILROY'S Travel Bureau

John Derry McIlroy was born into a family of five in Dumfries in 1894 and served with the Kings Own Scottish Borderers in the first world war. In 1923 in Belfast he married Eileen Mahony, a name to feature again later in the story. During the depression of the 1930s, they moved to Luton, living at 66 Chapel Street and later at 369 High Town Road. John served in both wars, as a sergeant-major in the Royal Engineers during WW2, and as part of the invasion forces, on the beaches during the D-Day landings.

John Derry McIlroy in 1964. (JM)

Although McIlroy's was the first travel bureau to open in Luton, John's first efforts at organizing excursions came when he was secretary of The Upside Down Track Social Club at Vauxhall Motors where he worked following his demobilisation. It fell to him to arrange the annual outing to Clacton or Margate, plus evening trips to London theatres or ice-hockey games. He was a very meticulous organizer, and the reward was usually a pat on the back and being re-elected for another year. He quickly realised there was a need for a business to organise such trips for everyone.

Firstly he advertised in "The Luton News" and then hired up to 12 coaches from Seamarks, Radio and other coach firms, offering return travel to south coast seaside destinations. He had a good response with confirmed bookings from enough families to fill all the coaches. On the Friday night there was a constant stream of people bringing their suitcases so that there was less for them to worry about on the Saturday morning of departure when, at 7.00am, the coaches left from New Street, Ebeneezer Street and Chapel Street. For the return trips family members always travelled down with the coaches and supervised the journey home. After everyone had returned home and the McIlroys had slowed down, John had a visit from a local police inspector who asked if he knew that a license was required for advertising for hire. In this case it was "ignorance is bliss", and please get a license next time!

There were many more next times, for John and his family went on to open their first public travel bureau at 88 Castle Street in 1947, and Lutonians were quick to avail themselves of the services offered. McIlroy's had agencies for freight and passenger railways with tickets at station prices, all principal air lines, holiday camps, London theatres, River Thames cruises, Canadian immigration and steamship travel. Especially popular was the London CERT, the Cheap Evening

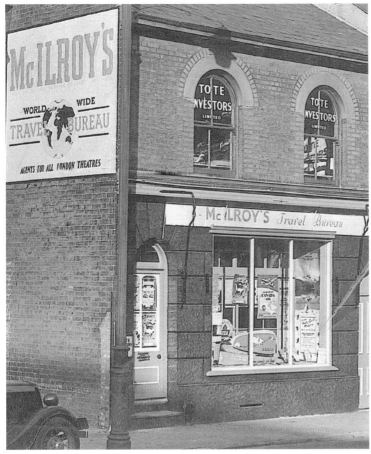

39 Waller Street, Luton c1950. (JM)

pennies and halfpennies. They were sent to the bank who telephoned to say that it was correct to the last penny. They also remember an enquiry to get a lady to Alaska where her husband was an engineer. There was no air travel, so two or three evenings were spent poring over timetables, sailing schedules on the Queen Mary, train connections across America and Canada and on to Alaska with a minimum of time and costs. An itinerary was finally produced to the lady when she called in at the bureau; however, she had called to say thank you, but her husband had been posted somewhere else and she would not be going after all.

About 1952, John was joined in business by his brother-in-law Joe Mahony who had moved to Luton from Sunderland. This did not prove to be a successful venture and caused friction and disharmony in the family. Eileen and John felt that all they could do was walk away from it, which they did in 1953. From this time the company name became Mahony's Travel Bureau. John was disappointed that his hard work in building up the business had disappeared without reward and for some time he worked as a progress chaser at Commer Cars. For ten years he was also

Return Ticket which covered the train, the tube and the theatre seat and cost just ten shillings.

As business expanded, a move was made in 1949 to additional premises at 39 Waller Street. It was an attractive shop with a large window usually filled with travel advertising, and there was a long counter so that three or four customers could be dealt with at once. John's family recall one of their first customers, Mr.Wenk, who had booked a passage to America on a Cunard liner and came in to pay with at least six biscuit tins full of

choirmaster at the Church of The Most Sacred Heart of Jesus in Ashcroft Road, Luton.

In 1962 Eileen and John emigrated to join their sons in New Zealand, and lived at Devonport on the North Shore of Auckland harbour. However, the entrepreneurial spirit was still alive and they bought a small bookshop and library at Cheltenham Beach. John also retained his first love with a job in the booking office for the Devonport Ferries. He finally retired when he reached 80 and moved to Wanganui near his son Joe. Eileen and John died, only four weeks apart, in 1981.

Interior of the travel bureau. (JM)

S. W. MANNING

In the 1930s snuff-takers in Luton knew where to go. Frances March's shop at 23 Cheapside was the meeting place for those interested in inhaling through the nostrils this preparation of powdered tobacco. It could be coloured, perfumed and be in a variety of moistures. In fashionable circles, smoking was giving way to this new craze. In 1938 when Frances sold her tobacconist's business, the recipe for her unique brand of snuff demanded and achieved an additional sum.

Sidney William Manning, a hat manufacturer in Reginald Street, seeing his trade vanish during the depression, decided to make a complete change, buying both the business and the valued snuff recipe. He continued to meet the demand, but having it produced by

Sidney Manning. (PM)

chemists Wootton & Webb in George Street. A quarter ounce sold for 1/6d (7 ¹/₂p) in a small triangular paper bag, but the menthol flavoured variety was more expensive. Sidney married Hilda Kilby, always known as Kibb, in 1918 originally living in Kenilworth Road, then in Reginald Street in the house which fronted the hat factory, and later Marsh Road. Now they moved in over the Cheapside shop and stayed there for 28 years, moving in retirement to Bedford Gardens in 1966. Sales were increased by incorporating the S. Atkins newsagency and greetings cards business from next door and extending the ground floor in 1959.

Richard Douglas, their son, had been born in 1919 and at the age of two met his future wife, Philippa Ward from Grove Road, their parents being good friends.

S.W. Manning at 23 Cheapside in 1939. (PM)

Dick Manning at the Cheapside counter. (PM)

organiser of the Football Charities. After a short illness Dick died in 1987, but Pip continues to live in Southwold near her two sons and seven grandchildren. The Mayor of Southwold described Dick as "A little gentleman in his shop, the children loved him and he had a cheery word for everybody".

Richard (Dick), attended Old Bedford Road School and Luton Modern School in Park Square, and Philippa (Pip) went to the Saint-Marie Convent School in Rothesay Road and Luton High School. They were eventually married at Christ Church and lived in Brantwood Road. Originally working at George Kent Ltd., Dick later joined his father in Cheapside where the business progressed until, like many Lutonians, their livelihood ended with the compulsory purchase of the premises in 1972. Sidney had continued walking morning and evening paper rounds right up until this time, when he was 82 years old.

Dick's last shop in Southwold. (SWo)

Pip and Dick moved to Southwold, where for 15 years they ran a successful confectionery and tobacconists shop in the High Street. Parents Sidney and Hilda joined them in Suffolk shortly after, but Sidney died four years later. Pip and Dick lived over the shop, from where Dick helped many local deserving causes as

LESLIE MARSHALL

"Today's unorthodoxy", the Prince of Wales told a meeting of the British Medical Council in 1982, "is probably tomorrow's convention". Since that time alternative therapies have become much more accepted, alternative practitioners often able to offer more time than busy doctors. Patients also appreciate healing by touch through massage, acupressure and other remedial treatments. All of this put Leslie Marshall M.C.S.P., S.R.P., F.R.S.H. very

Luton Building Company. A later job with a hat manufacturer resulted in dismissal for having carried the felts through the streets on a barrow and allowing them to get wet when it rained. In 1940 he married Peggy Land, moving into St. Monica's Avenue, their home for the next 57 years, and where they had two sons Barry and Nicholas. Leslie was now training to be a qualified toolmaker with the Davis Gas Stove Company in Dallow Road where he held an additional position as a first-aider. It was an initial interest and

Leslie was the physio (2nd from right) with the Bedfordshire County Youth football team in 1947. (NM)

much ahead of his time, for he was virtually self-taught and an enthusiastic believer and practitioner in homeopathy and electronic acupuncture long before 1982.

Leslie was born in Langley Street, Luton in 1913, his father being a grocer who at one time managed Sainsburys. He attended the Waller Street Schools and on leaving became an office-boy with the

subsequent training in this which was to form his life's work.

After the war Leslie began his professional practice in a room above "Tots & Teens" in Upper George Street. The top floor of the building was not occupied except for the resident ghost who was seen one day sitting in the waiting room before walking into the clinic and vanishing. In 1967 better premises were

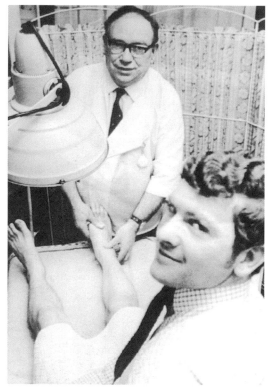

Leslie 'at work' with a patient. (NM)

taken in Gordon Chambers, above Barclays Bank on the opposite side of Upper George Street. Later moves were to New Bedford Road and Bury Park Road. Patients needing treatment were sent to him from Manor House Hospital in London and he also treated athlete Lillian Board and boxer Jack Dempsey, in addition to his loyal following of local patients.

Leslie Marshall was the official physiotherapist to Luton Town Cricket Club for 40 years, annually presenting a trophy in his name for the best young cricketer of the year. He was also physio for the Vauxhall Motors Football Club for some years. His outside interests were many and varied, being a member of the Lansdowne Club and the Co-op Golf Society. He had a share in a racing greyhound, and enjoyed membership of freemasonry in the Stockwood Lodge. He was Chairman for 13 years of the Luton & South Beds Committee for Cancer Relief, and received a certificate honouring his services from the National Society for Cancer Relief. Finally he was a piano player, by ear, who loved the opportunity to play in local pubs. His son Barry died at the age of 50. Nicholas, with his wife Margaret, are hosts at the Shallmarose Bed and Breakfast house in Clophill, Bedfordshire.

Leslie Marshall, Member of the Company of State Physiotherapists, State Registered Physiotherapist, Fellow of the Royal Society for Health and real 'character', died in March 1998, only three months after his wife Peggy. He was aged 85, and on his way to work! He had given kind-hearted, sympathetic, considerate and skilful treatment to the people of Luton at his Evandore Clinics for more than 50 years.

Leslie Marshall c1970. (NM)

The Merchant family came from Braughing in Hertfordshire. The link with Luton seems to go back to 1845 when William Walker, a baker from Braughing, whose wife was Eleanor Merchant, bought some land in the town.

going through on 4th December 1919 for the sum of £6151. 6s. 2d. The vendors were Horace and Neville Sworder, physician and solicitor respectively.

Francis and his wife Agnes had two sons, James and Frank. They were all partners in the firm until Frank's death in 1925. Frank and his wife had one son Charles who was also involved in the business. James married Maude Barford (from the firm of feltmakers, dyers and hatters in Luton and Bedford) and they had six children. The eldest, Herbert George, was being trained for the family business when, as Lieutenant George Merchant of the 9th Btn. attached 7th Btn.

Left to right, Francis Merchant, James Merchant, Leslie Merchant. (BT)

In 1855 Francis Merchant, a cabinet maker, founded the firm of house furnishers, with removals and storage, known as F. Merchant & Sons, later to become a limited company. From family documents, it seems that the property in Manchester Street was partly owned by Francis at that time with the final purchase

Bedfordshire Regiment, he was killed in 1916 in the Battle of the Somme, aged 22, and has no known grave. Four other children died in infancy as was so common in Victorian and Edwardian England. This left Leslie who was, at the time of George's death, a fifteen year old pupil at Bedford School with ideas of the

10 Manchester Street, Luton. (T.G. Hobbs)

ground, lower ground and first floors. Soft furnishings took you further back in the building, down some steps into the carpet and linoleum department, and then out of the back of the retail areas of the building. Here was the removals part of the business where the vans were stored, as well as repair and workshops, and the wonderful aroma of French polishing. Merchant's also incorporated the Luton Electric Carpet Beating Works, and made indoor and outdoor blinds. In 1900 they advertised that they had "two men, horse and large van for hire at 2/- (10p) an hour". Kathleen and Leslie's daughter Brenda recalls very clearly many of the people who worked there. "Mr. Honey was the foreman on removals, Mr. Sidney Box estimated the cost of removals, Mr. Peddar was the French polisher, Mr. Fisher was the chief carpet layer. Mrs. Brooker and Mrs. Allen made the loose covers. In the office I remember Mr. Haggie and Miss Purkis who dealt with the accounts and

Indian Civil Service or surgery as a career after university. Being the sole survivor of a family of six, it is easy to understand that he did not wish to rock the boat or make his parents' lives any more difficult in the circumstances, hence when he left Bedford School he went straight into training for the family business.

Leslie married Kathleen Farmer in 1935. She was the youngest daughter of Sidney Farmer who had a music business at 83 George Street, and also in Dunstable. Kathleen later became a director of Merchant's. Her elder sister, Connie, had married Percy Congreve who ran a hat manufacturing company in Union Street, Luton.

Merchant's ran back from 8-10 Manchester Street parallel with Williamson Street and Bridge Street, and there was a right-of-way between them and the adjacent property. There were showrooms on the

Enter the Hoover, Exit dirt and dust. Merchant's window display, c1912. (BT)

Betty Janes who did all the typing and answered the phone. And then there was the immaculate and ever courteous Mr. Gibbons, chief salesman and Leslie's right hand man, whose wife Jean had a florist's shop also in Manchester Street. I also recall that there was a man employed simply to open and close the door for customers".

James Merchant who had lived at 'Sweden Bank' in London Road, Luton, died in 1946 at the age of 83. He had been a church warden at Luton Parish Church for 25 years, and for his long service as Vicar's Warden was appointed to the position of Warden Emeritus. He was a founder member of Luton Rotary Club, later being made an honorary member, Canon Wm. Davison saying at his funeral that he lived up to the club's motto "Service above Self". He also likened him to Saint Barnabas, "a good man in a practical sense, generous and full of understanding, never seeking honour or praise." "He did not make money or success the goal of his life", said the vicar, "and those in his employ looked on him as a friend and father".

Leslie Merchant retired in 1960 after selling the business to Blundell Brothers, but retained ownership of the property until it was compulsorily purchased for redevelopment. It stood on what is now St. George's Square. Leslie and Kathleen had lived in Stockingstone Road, Luton for many years, moving to Toddington in 1962 and Kent in 1985. Leslie died in 1993, aged 91. His practical knowledge of the furnishing trade had served him in good stead during his wartime duties in the equipment branch of the RAF, with whom he had obtained a commission. He was a member of Luton Rotary Club for over 40 years and was president in 1952/3. He was also a warden and sidesman at Luton Parish Church, a scout leader and secretary and chairman of Luton Toc-H. He was active in the Conservative party, was a board member of Three Counties Hospital at Arlesey in Bedfordshire and a member of the local Review Committee of the National Parole Board.

Charles's sister Marjorie married an Italian Army officer before the Second World War and, at the age of 97, is still living in Rome. Leslie's daughter Brenda married Michael Turnbull who was senior curate at Luton Parish Church in the early 1960's, later becoming Bishop of Rochester in Kent. He is now the Bishop of Durham, and he and Brenda live in Bishop Auckland.

F. Merchant & Sons Ltd, whose motto was "Keep Moving", was part of a Luton that has long since disappeared. It stood for quality, standards and a level of service that would be hard to find today.

W. MOORING & SON

Walter Mooring was born on 7th January 1873 in the Bedfordshire village of Houghton Regis which at that time had only about 2,000 residents, of which a large majority made a profitable living in

45 Wellington Street, Luton. (AB)

the straw plaiting trade. Girls leaving school could be seen sitting outside their houses plaiting to assist the family income. This was not a job for boys, so when Walter left school at 13 he travelled into Luton every day to a shop in Park Street where he started as an apprentice in the boot and shoe trade.

At this time the sewing machine, which had marked an epoch in the manufacture of boots and shoes, was undergoing developments which lasted for the next fifty years. The final triumph came when it was adapted to the difficult work of sewing the upper to the thick heavy sole. With six years of learning his trade behind him, Walter was confident in his abilities as a cordwainer, and at the age of 20 set

up his own business at 62 Wellington Street. Later when he moved his premises to No.45 on the other side of the road, No.62 was occupied for many years by retail fish merchants, S.Gray.

On November 3rd 1897 Walter married Esther Lee who lived in London Road. They were both aged 24, and both of their fathers were gardeners. The wedding was conducted by Canon Thomas Bulman at St.Paul's Church, and in 1900 their son Arthur was born. When Arthur left school at 14, he joined his father at work, and in 1928 at Luton's Christ Church he married Winnie May Bass from Bury Park Road, and they set up home in Russell Rise. Winnie, who had been working in the millinery trade in London, also joined the flourishing W. Mooring & Son, expanding with Arthur the retail shoe sales. The company progressed in the face of keen multiple competition, specialising in the Wearra brand of shoes which offered slim, medium and broad fittings, and boasted that "A long life of silent service was built into every pair", and "Not a squeak nor a pinch from the very first". Men's middleweight Oxfords, "the all-occasion favourite" sold for 69/11, (£3.49) and ladies sandal shoes "ideal for a brilliant or indifferent summer" cost 49/11 (£2.49).

The enterprise continued to grow, providing that service which is the prerogative of the private retailer. Set in one of Luton's main shopping streets, it became the oldest established shoe retailing business in the town. Walter was an acknowledged expert in bespoke boot and shoe making, specialising in surgical boots for hospitals, and also in the busy repair department.

Walter and Esther lived in Caddington for nearly 40 years, calling their home Wellingtonia. He was Vicar's Warden for 25 years, and a Churchwarden for 33 years. He was also a sergeant in the 3rd Bedfordshire Volunteer Force and played trombone in the 5th Bedfordshire Regimental Band. He was a founder member of the Luton British Legion Club and for many years served in the Luton Special Constabulary, being on duty during the riots of 1919. In addition he was a member of the local Tradesmens Association, before it became known as the Chamber of Trade. Arthur Mooring also became prominent in the business life of Luton serving as President of The Luton & District Chamber of Trade. He was also Treasurer at Christ Church for many years.

Walter, Arthur and Winnie remained active in their business until its closure in 1964, when the wine and spirit merchants Greeners moved into No.45, now the tandoori restaurant Shapla.

Walter Mooring using a Blake Sewer for bespoke shoe making on the premises, about 1930. (AB)

Walter died in November 1966 at the age of 93 after more that 75 years connection with the Luton shoe trade. Arthur died in 1986. Winnie lived very happily close to her daughter and son-in-law on the Isle of Wight for many years but died in 2002.

Winnie and Arthur Mooring. (AB)

F. H. MOSS (GARAGES)

William Moss, civil engineering contractors of Loughborough and London, were a prominent company at the beginning of the last century, one important contract being the building of Loughborough College. William's son Charles was also part of the business, but

The Moss family, left to right, Irene, Ralph, William, Bruce, Richard, Frank. (BMo)

sale on 31st March 1928 was a used Douglas motorcycle which he had bought for £25 on 6th March and sold to a customer from Dane Road, Luton for £30. Enfields, Zeniths, Rudges, Ariels, BSA and AJS all appear in sales at that time. This site is now the University of Luton bookshop. In 1938 a move was made further along Park Street where private houses were demolished and the new F.H. Moss garage and workshop were built at No's 53 to 61. New and second-hand motorcycles and sidecar combinations were bought and sold, and Morgan sports cars also became very popular. Family models sold for £80/16/3 (£80.81), the Aero-M for £108/0/9 (£108.04) but the Saloon version fetched £131/12/6 (£131.63).

his son Frank Henry is the subject of this essay. Born at Chippendale House, Barrow, in the County of Leicester in 1904, Frank was sent to Tonbridge School in Kent. It was following this that his enthusiasm for motorcycles became apparent, and he could often be seen racing his Brough Superior. His business life commenced with a small garage and forecourt at Elstree in Hertfordshire and then at Camberley where he gained the Austin agency.

The Luton story begins in 1928 when he opened his first local garage at 39e Park Street, "confident" he said "that it was a town which would grow". Frank's sales records still exist and show that his first

Some Morgans were tuned in the workshop for owners who raced them at the Brooklands Racing Circuit. In 1931 Frank won the London to Edinburgh Trial in a Morgan, and the next year he held the unofficial British motorcycle land speed record, but only for two weeks! His prowess on the racing track and his energy in building his garage business brought success, but he slipped up one day when visiting Hitchin market where he bought a motorcycle which seemed to be running smoothly, intending it for resale. It got him no further than Offley Hill, and had to be collected by the garage where it was found that its single piston was made of wood!

Dick's first vintage Bentley, which he still drives, in the garage entrance in 1959. (BMo)

Bruce controlled the company accounts and Ralph supervised the workshop which, during the war, was heavily involved in engineering for the Royal Navy. Main agencies for Standard and Triumph cars were held, and later Fiat and Lancia, also the respected marques of Alfa-Romeo and Jaguar. Next door to the garage and cornering Vicarage Road, an empty house was used for storage of motor oils. A branch garage was opened in Ampthill in 1962, but was sold after only three years.

During the 1950's Bill Moss became recognized as one of the country's leading young drivers racing many historic vehicles at Silverstone, Alton Park and Brands Hatch. He raced the R1A, the first ERA car built,

In 1932 at East Hyde Church near Luton, Frank married Irene Burgess. Irene's brother Robin was proprietor of the Speedwell Factoring Co. which was to the rear of Partridge's cycle shop in Chapel Street, Luton.

Irene and Frank had four sons, William, Richard, Ralph and Bruce, their births spanning ten years, and all entering the family business after schooling and university. The family moved into 109 London Road, Luton in 1948. At the garage Bill was in charge of vehicle sales, and indeed the author recalls buying his first car from Bill, a second-hand 1948 Flying Standard-12. Its sunshine roof leaked and my seat had to be supported with a broomstick, but it was eight years old and still gave us a great deal of pleasure. Dick and

Interior of the garage workshop during World War 2. (BMo)

and with the later 'Remus' won almost every event he entered. A 1929 Aston Martin DB3S followed in vintage events,

---

111

and later a Lister-Jaguar. All of these successful cars were prepared at the Park Street garage. Bill went on to join the Gemini Racing Team driving professionally in the Formula Junior events. He became Junior Champion for one year and in

Bill taking a tight bend. (BMo)

Remus also the Junior Hill Climb Champion. Remus had originally cost £700, but at auctions now ERA cars sell for half a million pounds. Sadly his racing career ended with a serious accident during a race at Rheims in France.

Frank retired in 1972 to further his enjoyment of yachting and his new home at Hill Farm House in Barton le Cley, and the next few years saw the family moving away from this well-known Luton garage. Bill left to open motor engineers Hire-A-Bay in Bilton Way, Luton where the public could service their cars in well-equipped bays, and later retired to Tetbury in Gloucestershire. Dick formed his own company, Richard Moss Ltd. at Bolnhurst in Bedfordshire, and still specialises in restoring and rebuilding vintage Bentley motor cars. In 1972 the F. H. Moss garage was sold to Mann Egerton who, within a year, were themselves to become part of Donald Stokes' British Leyland empire. Agencies were then transferred to Dunham & Haines in Luton, and Moss's garage was closed down and demolished. The site is now the Iceland foodstore. A year later Ralph and Bruce opened their family business which still flourishes selling quality antiques from a showroom in Baldock.

Both Irene and Frank died in a fatal accident following a head-on collision on the road between Hitchin and Hexton in 1982. Their name lives on in their sons' businesses and will not be forgotten, for Moss's in Park Street, Luton was a name of high repute in car sales locally for 44 years.

G.H. NORMAN

I suppose it was almost an inborn presumption that I would spend my working life behind the counter, with both a father and grandfather who had done so

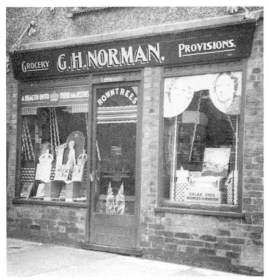

25 Letchworth Road declares "A health unto their majesties" in 1937.

been about two or three. Dad, a Stevenage boy, had been a policeman and a Lyons Tea salesman before we took over the Letchworth Road shop, moving from 14 Fitzroy Avenue, where I had been born. He had also been a cartoonist with the Hertfordshire Express, specialising in football cartoons depicting the games and caricatures of the players of Stevenage Town F. C. We stayed in Limbury throughout the war years until 1945 when Grandad died, and we moved once again into his vacated shop, this time at no.1 Lyndhurst Road.

The shop in Limbury where I spent my childhood can best be described as being very much like that in the television series 'Open All Hours'. It had the same layout, the same bare well-swept wooden floor, and in the same way seemed to sell almost everything; Dad even wore the same brown overall. I remember deep wooden drawers containing loose flour, sugar, dried fruit and rice, each with a large scoop and strong brown paper bags

before me, Dad having twice followed his father-in-law into the same shop. Born a Londoner, and originally a master baker in Hitchin, grandad William Charles Minnis went into his general store at 25 Letchworth Road, Luton on the corner with Norton Road about 1930. He stayed there for about four years, moving then into a confectionary and tobacconist's shop at 1 Lyndhurst Road on the corner with Dallow Road. As he moved out of Letchworth Road, we moved in; I must have

"We sell Lyons Ice Cream" states the board outside 1 Lyndhurst Road in 1948.

being used for customers' orders. Below the drawers were wooden bins for potatoes and other vegetables, and one morning job I had was to check the mousetraps placed here for any overnight occupants. It seems very surprising now but it was also standard practice to check the rice draw for black 'rice' from overnight visitors! Butter and cheese were kept under wire-framed muslin covers on marble slabs on the counter, and I recall rolling the large cheesecloth wrapped cheddars from the storeroom into the shop, and also Dad showing me how to bone a side of bacon ready for placing on the slicer. Medical supplies were stocked; I particularly recall the demand for Carter's Little Liver Pills, Gregory and Beechams Powders, and also Ex-Lax which the poster on the window tells us 'ends incomplete elimination'. It certainly did that. There was a good selection in the sweet counter even then (sherbert fountains, parma violets, black jacks, sugar false teeth etc.) Stockings and tablecloths hung on a broomstick which was suspended horizontally over this counter. Shelves behind the counters reached up to the ceiling displaying castor oil, Colman's starch, Dolly Blue, Silvo, Brasso and Zambuk, it was seemingly endless. The house and shop were always full of stock, but Dad knew where everything was. I have never been too fond of spiders, possibly since discovering a huge hairy one in a crate of fruit. One pocket-money perk I had was collecting and selling the apples which had fallen from the trees in the garden. Under these trees was the entrance to our air-raid shelter which was large enough to share with neighbours, and in which I recall sleeping through many nights. We even sold paraffin from a large drum in the garden, where in a shed we also charged accumulators for customers who used them in their wirelesses. I can remember boxes of loose nails, gas mantles, candles, Aladdin globes and wicks for Hurricane lamps. Hickmans delivered fresh bread daily, and greengrocery was supplied by Dick Higgs from his smallholding at Westoning. During the war I spent many evenings helping to count almost every ration coupon that existed, bundling them up for later delivery to the Food Office. Goods were shown in both money and ration points, everyone having a points allowance. Some items, however, were on full ration, being a fixed monthly allowance. Customers had to decide which grocer to register with, our competitors in that area being the Co-op and Mr. Fuller's shop in Limbury Road. Dad did well in this respect and was always very fair with items which were in short supply, keeping a list so that registered customers took their turn to be able to buy such scarce items as a bottle of tomato ketchup.

Mum and Dad had friends in a similar business, Mr. & Mrs. Petitt whose shop was in Connaught Road , Luton, on the corner with Beverley Road, and they had a son John of the same age as myself. On Sunday mornings, before the war, the six of us would travel to the Houndsditch Warehouse Company in London where goods were purchased for resale in the shops. John and I are still good friends, and we recall with pleasure these days out in Mr. Petitt's Hillman Minx when we used to stand in the rear of the car holding on to the front seats. We must have been about five years old.

The move from Limbury to Lyndhurst Road took place when I was 13, and it was into a high-class confectioner's and tobacconist's shop, for Grandad had always stocked high-quality sweets when they were available. I think there was no rival to the British sweet shop when barley sugars and boiled sweets were shaken noisily into the scales from large glass jars, and then tipped into paper bags, before being twirled over and over to seal the corners. Both Grandad, and later Dad, were proud to sell confectionery by Pascalls, Frys and by Fred Needler of Hull, especially their chocolate bon-bons. Nuttall's Mintoes were popular, also Parkinson's Butterscotch from Doncaster. Bluebird or Palm toffee was broken from large slabs using a small hammer, which I still have. I recall with pleasure the day Dad had a refrigerator installed in the shop and Lyons Ice Cream was once again on sale, announced outside as 'cooling news'. This shop had a unique doorbell which comprised a weight on the doorframe falling across a box on the door which contained four bars, giving a doh-ray-me-fah on opening, and a fah-me-ray-doh when closed. Pipe tobaccos, cigars and cigarettes were also sold in quantity in those days. Names that stay in mind are St.Bruno flake, Digger, Kensitas, Craven-A and Turf. Both our shop premises have changed considerably

in appearance over the years. The Letchworth Road site is now the offices of internet company Camelot International, and 1 Lyndhurst Road has become Sandhu's Launderette.

Both Mum and Dad served in their shop until retirement to a bungalow in Gooseberry Hill, Luton in 1965. Sadly the smaller shops are becoming backups for the larger supermarkets and find it difficult to survive on casual trade only. Fifty years ago corner shops such as ours were convenient and very often successful, many like them offering a competitive alternative to the town centre shops.

George Norman, ready to serve.

G.T.OSBORN

Godfrey Thomas Osborn was born the son of a butcher in Olney, Buckinghamshire in 1899. This was also to be his chosen trade, for in the early 1920's he came as a young man to work for Mr.W. Panter, the family butcher and game dealer, at 34-36 Park Street in Luton.

cellar turkeys were plucked and drawn before sale. It was a family concern, father-in-law Walter Page who lived at 72 Dudley Street being the slaughterman and often seen carrying sides of beef on his shoulders the 25 yards along the road from the cold store. Merchandise was fresh every morning with special displays for the weekend and especially at Christmas. A cheerful service was always given in the

Christmas 1941 at 133 Albert Street. Left to right, Hilda Jude (Cashier), Pamela Osborn, Godfrey Osborn, Gladys Osborn, Horace Bates, Alfred, Reg O'Dell. (JF)

It was here that he met his future wife, Gladys Page.

In the late 1920s they bought their own business at 133 Albert Road, Luton on the corner with Baker Street. Early every Tuesday, 'Goff' as he was usually known, would travel to Hitchin market to buy game for resale in his shop. His staff were always busy making sausages and pork pies on the premises, where in the

butcher's shop, with the sawdust-covered floor, the scrubbed chopping blocks behind the counter and the staff always in their freshly ironed white aprons. There was a much appreciated delivery service available when, before the purchase of a van, assistants filled the bulky wicker baskets on the front of their bicycles before cycling off to their customers.

Master butcher Goff Osborn became

Freddie Rance on the butcher's box cart. On the right on horseback is Patricia Mossman. (JF)

President of the Luton & District Butchers Association in 1960, but six years later the business was sold on to Mr. F. Chaney. The family home at Woodside, near Luton, was a stables and farm overflowing with pigs, chickens and his greatest love, horses. At weekends he could often be seen at local shows driving his butcher's box-cart with his favourite hackney horse Billy. Retirement was spent here, where he died in 1988.

Godfrey Osborn. (JF)

W.H.PALMER

Can you believe that one of the most colourful characters in the world of jazz walked through Luton looking for a cup of tea? It happened.... read on.

Originally a private house occupied by Henry Thrussell, No.7 Waller Street was, for almost sixty years, the premises of W.H. Palmer, they having previously been

No. 7 Waller Street, Luton. (RJe)

in Cheapside. At their head-office in Old Street, London, Walter Palmer had manufactured paints and French polishes since 1805 and varnishes of a high strength were produced in their factory at Clapham. The quality resulted from their process in which the varnish matured in huge vats for eleven years before use. Three types of methylated spirits were produced and sold; industrial, surgical and the mineralised type which had the blue tint added to enable the public to

know that it was not water and, therefore, not to drink it. All of these products were on sale in Waller Street.

Palmer's satisfied a local demand from the hat trade where gelatine was used for stiffening. Catherine Booth, the wife of the founder of the Salvation Army, designed their bonnet with a strong wide brim to protect against bricks and stones which were thrown at them in their early days. Palmers imported a stronger Belgian type for use in the production of these bonnets, which had to be stiffened to the point where they could withstand being sat upon without collapsing. Many of their products were sold locally to Gibbs & Dandy and Ogden & Cleaver and to chemists for resale, and also to local hospitals. Pure white gelatine had a very different use when it was sold to Rudds to be used in the production of their pork pies.

The Luton branch was managed from 1908 to 1944 by Lutonian Oliver Dawson, who was engaged in tea importing until a friendship with a member of the Palmer family gained him this position. From 1944 until demolition in 1967, it was managed by Ron Jeakings. Born in Clifton Road, Luton in 1911, Ron came from the Jeakings family of fruiterers, and went to Dunstable Road School where he found an interest in music. Later he played banjo, guitar, clarinet and saxophone with the Sydney Phasey Orchestra in the ballroom, stage and pit of the Alma Theatre. Here, on Saturdays,

Ron Jeakings stands proudly in front of their large paint stock. (RJe)

musicians, then walked along George Street to Edwards Restaurant in Manchester Street for tea and cakes!

W.H. Palmer had large sales of their own brand paint, bright yellow cans bearing the name Paglos. In addition they were agents for the sale of Walpamur, Luxol and Magicote paints, with many hundreds of gallons always in stock. They had a strong business in the town until the arrival of the large D.I.Y. superstores, and the decline of the local hat trade. At closure the goodwill was purchased by G.F. Farr Ltd.

Ron Jeakings is still resident in Luton, but unfortunately now on his own, his wife having died recently.

dances were held in the tea-room. He performed in the George Hotel Ballroom when Albert Coupe, later to conduct the Luton Band, was first trumpet. Also with the Geoff Stokes Orchestra when they were resident at The George. But he remembers with pride playing in the early 1930s as part of the St. Louis Players backing a young Louis Armstrong in the Waller Street Winter Assembly Hall as part of an evening arranged by hat manufacturer Denis Wright. Amazingly Ron, together with the legendary Satchmo and the other

The St. Louis Players at the Palace Theatre in Mill Street, Luton in the 1930's. Ron is 3rd from the right. (RJe)

SHANKS & TURNER

Two members of Luton Town Football Club once made their own retail sports shop in Luton as memorable as their abilities on the field. They were Wally Shanks and Gordon Turner, who were joined by their friend Jack Edge.

Jack and Wally originated the business, doing boot repairs and selling footballs at 109/111 Bury Park Road. Before joining his colleagues, Gordon was a sales representative for G.A. Wild & Sons, and of course he and Wally were busy elsewhere on Saturday afternoons!! In 1960 the company, now Shanks & Turner, moved to 123 Dunstable Road, where they stayed for the next 13 years.

Wally Shanks and Gordon Turner. (MT)

Luton's first new pedestrianised shopping area, the West Side Centre, built on the site of the old gasworks, came into being in 1972 and Wally & Gordon moved into Unit 36. This was their most successful venture, holding all the main agencies including Umbro, Adidas and Puma, and generous discounts were offered to all Sports Clubs. Both Wally with his wife Anne and Gordon with his wife Margaret were living in Stoneygate Road.

Trade was good but, when the Arndale Centre came into being, passing trade at the West Side Centre was very much reduced. In addition to this, both the families and the company suffered a painfully sad loss when in 1976, Gordon Turner, suffering from motor neurone disease, died at the age of 46. A further move of the shop was then made to 38 George Street, the vacant Freeman, Hardy & Willis shoe shop which is now occupied by the Lunn Poly Holiday Shop. Business was good at first, but with local rate increases, a staff of eight to support and their suppliers now selling in quantity to superstores, it became less viable to continue. In 1981 Sportsday Ltd. took the business over, but were successful for only a short period.

Gordon Turner's son Michael is in business in Luton as Serenade Windows, and his eldest son Mark who bears a striking resemblance to his grandfather, proudly displays Gordon's football shirts in his bedroom. Gordon's widow Margaret, and Anne and Wally Shanks still live in the town.

This final paragraph must surely note the football facts. Wally Shanks came to Luton from Chelsea F.C. in 1947. He was a most versatile player, eventually becoming chief coach and serving Luton Town for 13 years. Gordon Turner was the son of a former Hull City professional, played for Doncaster boys and joined Luton Town from the Navy. In the No. 8 shirt he played through the Club's glorious days of the late 1950s, making 406 appearances.

'The Rover', a footballing magazine of the '50s, always carried pictures of famous footballers on its front page, and there in 1955 alongside an equally young Bobby Robson is Gordon Turner. He scored 276 goals in his 14 years career and his Club record of 243 goals in the League still stands. Roger Wash, dedicated Hatters historian and author who lived in Ivy Road as a boy, recalls taking his footballs into the Shanks and Turner shop nearby and Gordon Turner instructing him in the correct way to lace them.

Luton Town FC. Both in the front row, Gordon is 2nd from left, and Wally is 2nd from right. (MT)

Shaw & Kilburn

Shaw and Kilburn was for 64 years known to Lutonians as the local Vauxhall-Bedford franchise. They were, in fact, the country's largest Vauxhall-Bedford dealers, yet it all started as a shell factory close to Piccadilly Circus!

When Henry Shaw and Drysdale Kilburn decided to enter the retail motor

Shaw and Mr. Kilburn decided to turn their building into a temporary factory making shells and aircraft parts. Eventually 700 staff were turning out 5,000 shells a week, and all within 400 yards of Piccadilly Circus! In peacetime the premises were converted to the sales and servicing of a newly acquired agency, the American Hudson motor car, and in 1920 they also became Vauxhall dealers. Additional premises were found in Conduit Street, and two years later they purchased The Grosvenor Carriage

Hand building Vauxhalls in Shaw & Kilburn's first acquisition, The Grosvenor Carriage Co. in 1922. (BP)

business they found ideal premises in London's Wardour Street, but unfortunately the year was 1917 and World War I was at its height. So Mr.

Company at the Welbeck Works in Kimberley Road, Willesden, who were body-builders of high repute, producing motor cars with aluminium frame and

The site for the new Shaw & Kilburn garage at 546-550 Dunstable Road, Luton in 1930. (BP)

wings on wooden ash bodies. Business prospered and in 1925, the year that General Motors took over Vauxhall, Shaw & Kilburn opened new London premises in Dean Street backing onto those in Wardour Street. The two were linked so that motorists could drive into 114 Wardour Street and leave by 75 Dean Street, "or vice versa" added an advertisement of the time.

The five-storey premises in the heart of London's theatreland created favourable comment in the society and motoring press, and even in 1925 with relatively few vehicles on the road, the Sunday Times complained that "the garaging of a car in the centre of a crowded city is always a problem". Shaw & Kilburn's new premises solved that with accommodation for 800 cars and the largest car lift in London. There were six dressing rooms, three for gentlemen and three for ladies, and also a chauffeur's room provided with illustrated papers.

During 1925 Shaw & Kilburn began to expand outside London, and their first acquisition bought this respected name to Luton. In this year they purchased West End Motors from its owner Mr. Bill Powers who, in his younger days, had been a Vauxhall Motors apprentice and also served as a mechanic in the Royal Naval Air Service in World War I. They were at 233 Dunstable Road, between Oak Road and Ash Road, and at this time advertised that "our hire car is the most comfortable and reliable in the district". Bill Powers was to remain with the company for the next 30 years, becoming its Assistant Managing Director. His grandfather Percy had been a deputy judge in Luton in 1895, and lived in Brantwood Road. Bill was born there but later lived at 19 Claremont Road, and for many years at The Glade at 570 Dunstable Road. Premises in Warwick Road were developed in 1934, but two years later the Company acquired 546-550 Dunstable Road, where they built the most up-to-date garage in Bedfordshire, yet Powdrills, the Luton builders suppliers, were still using a horse and cart to transport materials to the site. Promoting the company at this time, a demonstration convoy of Vauxhall DX and DY models showing the wide variety of bodies which could be built onto them went from Wardown Park through the town centre, headed by a miniature car specially built for the occasion by Shaw & Kilburn and driven by Bill Powers.

On Monday 1st November 1937, Shaw & Kilburn opened Luton's most modern service station and showrooms on their new 7 acre site. The tower on the building boasted a clock which was eventually replaced with the company shield because so many people complained that it was never correct. As Vauxhall and Bedford main dealers for our area, they were equipped with special plant and employed factory-trained mechanics, advertising that

The Mayor of Luton, Ald. J.T. Harrison with Bill Powers Snr. in a 1905 Vauxhall at the opening of the new garage in 1937. (BP)

they offered "service with knowledge". At this time the vacated premises at 233 Dunstable Road became Luton Car Mart and later W. T. Parrott & Co. In 1939 the new premises were taken over by the government who, for the period of the war, used them as an army vehicle workshop. In peacetime the company continued to expand its business and in the 1950s it was acquired by Sears Holdings, one of Britain's largest groups which also included Selfridges, Saxone, Garrards, Mappin & Webb and The British

The oil and grease bay in the S. & K. service centre. (BP)

The new garage and service centre in 1962. (BP)

Shoe Corporation. After contracting cancer Bill Powers died in 1958. However a second Bill Powers, his nephew of the same name, continued to advance the company further, from the position of General Manager. Bill was the son of Doris and John Powers of Blenheim Crescent. John played the saxophone and was leader of the dance band known as Jack Powers and the Jovials. The biggest dance band in the county throughout the 1920s, they played in the main dance hall of the time, Ward's Restaurant in New Bedford Road, which later became the site for the Luton Co-operative Society store. He also played with some of the top London bands, including the Savoy Hotel Band, and during the war led the SKF Orchestra in Luton. Bill's brother Peter became S & K Service Manager and held responsibility for body and paint work, giving a total of 42 years service.

In 1963, on the opposite side of Dunstable Road on the corner with Chaul End Lane, Autorama was formed as the Used Car Division. This purpose-built site included a fully equipped workshop and a petrol station offering five grades of Esso petrol at reduced prices. In 1973 a £250,000 extension to the premises doubled the size of the old showrooms, the new parts and accessories department becoming nearly three times bigger than before and £50,000 worth of new testing equipment was installed. At this time the Luton centre became Head Office of the Shaw & Kilburn Organisation which had branches throughout the British Isles, the Managing Director in these years being Mr. R. Reid Jack, the Scottish international golfer. The opening ceremony for the new buildings was jointly performed by comedian Eric Morecambe and Hank Clark, Director of Sales at Vauxhall

Motors. The Mayor and Mayoress of Luton, Cllr. and Mrs. James McGrath, and the Mayor and Mayoress of Dunstable, Ald. and Mrs. E. Royce attended, together with the entire Luton Town football team with their Manager Harry Haslam. A joint competition with the South Beds Golf Club enabled members and friends to try and win a Vauxhall VX4/90 car for having achieved a hole-in-one. The Luton organisation eventually had 240 employees, and achieved annual sales of over 2,000 new cars and about 3,500 used cars.

A paragraph here must record the part that the second Bill Powers, Luton's very own Action Man, played in the life of our town. Born in Naseby Road, Luton in 1924, he can recall the trams running past his first school in Dunstable Road, and also being taken with his class outside the school to cheer the new maroon coloured Luton Corporation buses as they passed. He later saw war service as a Major in Number 9 Commando unit. In addition to his time with Shaw & Kilburn and as District Sales Manager with Vauxhall Motors, he became Group Manager for the Sears Group in London and eventually Principal of the Sears Motor Group with an annual turnover of £45M. For three years he gave business management lectures at Queens College and St. Catherine's College in Cambridge. Locally he was the County Organiser for the Queen's Silver Jubilee Appeal, held a Ministry of Defence appointment as Chairman of the USAF base at Chicksands, served as High Sheriff of Bedfordshire in 1988, as deputy to the Lord Lieutenant of

Bill Powers M.B.E. (BP)

Bedfordshire in 1989, and was appointed Chairman of South Bedfordshire Community Health Care Trust in 1990. The Luton Musical Pageant was his responsibility for 20 years and he was a member of Luton North Rotary Club. He was Deputy Chairman of Luton Magistrates Court for 15 years, and remains a Justice of the Peace, President of Dunstable Operatic Society, and has been the President of Luton Royal British Legion since the death of Sir Harold Wernher in 1960. Though no longer resident locally, he frequently travels back to his home town Luton, especially on each Remembrance Day to "recite the exhortation, and shout and stamp about as Parade Commander!" Although he has retired three times, he is currently Managing Director of The Old Vicarage Nursing Home in the beautiful Norfolk village of Ludham where he is responsible for 31 residents and 55 staff.

The Lex Motor Group bought 34 garages, including Shaw & Kilburn, within the Sears Organisation in 1989, but sold on for quick profit after only a short time.

Vauxhall dealers Pinnacle occupy the Autorama site, and the Shaw & Kilburn area is now both the Daewoo Service and Parts Centre, and PC-World.

VAUXHALL

*L*OCAL ENTERPRISES PROSPER

when they genuinely serve the needs of the community in which they are established. Shaw & Kilburn have faithfully served local needs for a generation and more—always with integrity and that quick personal interest in little jobs and special requirements that makes all the difference. Shaw & Kilburn sell and service local products too—cars and commercial vehicles built by Vauxhall Motors Ltd. And Vauxhall's own local tradition of quality in automobile engineering goes back half a century.

SHAW *and* KILBURN Ltd.

LUTON, LONDON, AYLESBURY, AMPTHILL, BERKHAMSTED

SNOWDENS

The business of A.T. Snowden occupied 171 Dunstable Road, Luton in 1932, originally being listed as wireless traders. Later they were known as electrical engineers and finally as radio and television dealers. Arthur Snowden also had premises at 24 Mill Street and 30

it experienced financial difficulties and went into receivership. Mr. Hubert Barlow of accountants Leeds, Barlow & Co. at 66 Alma Street, Luton was the official receiver. The company was jointly purchased at this time by Ronald Coe and Karl Jackson.

To continue this story we must go to Suffolk, where in 1914 Ronald was born to Alice and Elijah Coe at the Sudbury Police Station. Ron jokes that he is unsure if he started the war or if the war started

171 Dunstable Road, Luton about 1960. (RC)

New Bedford Road where he advertised that installations were undertaken for power, heat and light. He was the local "Pye" service agent and also agent for Gambrell, Red Star and Kolster-Brandes receivers. In 1931 a Pye twin-triple portable receiver for both battery and mains cost 22gns.(£23.05). He ran his shop on the Dunstable Road/ Kenilworth Road corner for 22 years until 1954, when

him! He does not remember his policeman father who died in 1917 from complications following his brave attempt to rescue people trapped in a building after a Zeppelin raid on the town. Ron lived with his paternal grandparents in Bardwell until the age of ten, when he was boarded at a police orphanage in Redhill, Surrey. He was able to return home two years later when his mother re-married,

Ronald Coe. (RC)

another policeman Robert Taylor, and they lived in the Police Station at Clare in Suffolk, where Douglas was born in 1923. Ron's entrepreneurial life began working for the Co-op, which was before he left school at the age of 14, later working for a Mr. Crow whose small premises were the telephone exchange, the post office, a shoeshop and the local labour exchange. With police retirement, the family moved to live in London Road, Clacton-on-Sea, where Ron gained a position with Broadcast Relay. This was significant in bringing Ron Coe to Luton, for in 1936 he was sent to install overhead cables in our town for the company's two-station wireless relays. He set up the signal

amplifier in Queen Square whilst living nearby in Queen Street. After experience as a bus conductor with the Eastern National Omnibus Company, he joined local electrical contractors Shoolbred at 1/3 Langley Street during which time he completely rewired Blundell Brothers premises.

In 1938 at Holy Trinity Church in Limbury Road, the Revd. Shewring married Ron to Ruby Ilott. They had met whilst shopping in the Luton Co-op store in New Bedford Road and they set up home in Beaumont Road. Ruby was born and lived next door to the Jolly Topers public house in Round Green. She recalls that there was a knacker's yard to the rear of their house, and also that their neighbour's garden went right along to Felix Avenue where St. Christopher's Church stands today. Wartime saw Ron serving as an armament staff sergeant with the Army in Italy and later working on defence systems to counteract the V1 "dooodlebugs" in Kent.

Back in Civvy Street in 1946, and now living in Abbey Drive, Ron saw progress on the business front, firstly selling radios and washing machines on a franchise basis by hiring Dillingham's Biscot Road shop window, and in 1949 moving into the first shop of his own, a new unit on Hockwell Ring, Luton where they lived above. It traded as Barons, an amalgam of his own christian name and that of his son Barry. Firstly selling hardware it also became successful in radio sales and the Coronation year of 1953 really began television sales. Barons sold fifty television sets prior to this event, a large number in those days, often working until 2 a.m. erecting aerials.

Now we can return to 1954 when Snowdens was purchased. This was a much larger premises with record, radio, television, washing machine and refrigerator sales and servicing departments. Sid Ilott was in charge of service and Bill Banks dealt with electrical installations, about 100 electricians and apprentices being employed at this time. A number of these

Douglas Taylor. (DT)

were usually at the Vauxhall Motors plant, especially during the July holiday break when it was customary for the production track to be completely rearranged, often for a new model, with the attendant electrical wiring it necessitated. Many television and radio agencies were acquired, some names seldom seen nowadays; Murphy, Philips, Sobell, Marconi, Peto Scott, Mullard, Decca, AEG and Grundig. Ron's half-brother, Doug Taylor joined as showroom manager in 1955, and indeed when the author was getting married recalls buying his first radiogram from him, a Peto Scott. Doug Taylor was later to form his own successful company, Lorell Photographics, now in Oakley Road, Luton and the author was later to spend thirteen very happy and successful years with him as his manager!

A.T. Snowden (Luton) Ltd. was registered as the company name, and in time Paramount Rentals was formed to extend the services offered. This in turn required finance, so a hire-purchase and rental finance company, Paramount Securities, was added to the group, along with the original Barons in Leagrave. A very successful business had been formed, but the pressure of work resulted in medical problems for Ron who left his company in 1969. However, he went on to be Accounts Director with H. F. Scriven in Bute Street, Luton, then to be a control panel manufacturer in Watford and later to be a design engineer with Honeywell Controls in 1971, finally retiring in 1979.

Snowdens was sold by Karl Jackson to Ketts, who also had a similar shop at 72/74 George Street, retaining the respected name of Snowdens on the premises until 1979. It is now Nasons General Store, an English and Asian food shop, and also the British Muslim Welfare Office. Arthur Snowden emigrated to South Africa but later returned to England. Ron Coe has been part of local Freemasonry for the past 41 years, now holding the position of Past Provincial Junior Grand Warden in the Warden Lodge.

He was also Chairman of the Caravan Club Bedfordshire Centre for a large part of his 30 years membership. Ruby and Ron, now in their mid-80s and not enjoying the best of health, moved many times in later years; Harpenden, Wokingham, Chesham, and Wellingborough but are now settled in Flitwick.

The Bute Street shop in 1940. (PW)

Bookbinder Samuel Bailey's printing press and shop at 12 Bute Street makes its first appearance in Luton records in 1881. Ten years later John Staddon who came from the Channel Island of Guernsey took over the business, having previously been a manager in London. His son Arthur joined him later, and the firm of J. Staddon & Son was born. The shop was also known as 'The Library' for there was an active book lending interest until the middle of the First World War. An indenture exists between employer John Staddon and apprentice George Warner for printing and cheque book binding in which the agreed wages for the first year (1893) was three shillings (15p) rising to twelve shillings (60p) in the seventh year. The company had further interests in die-stamping and engraving, and had good connections with local churches and education authorities.

In 1904, on the death of his father, control passed to Arthur Staddon. Although civic affairs did not attract him, he was a member of the Dunstable Downs Golf Club, the first Captain of Luton Town Bowling Club and a loyal member of Freemasonry as a steward in the Cumberland Lodge. He was responsible for the basement excavations in Bute Street to enable the housing of the printing machines in 1907, and replacing the original double-fronted shop windows just prior to 1914. He lived for some years at 'Cordova' in Holly Street before moving to a new house in New Bedford Road where he died in 1938, after 47 years trading in Bute Street. The interest passed to his wife who took little active part in the business which was virtually managed by two employees Miss E. M. Simpson and Mr. John Blagg. Alfred Staddon, Arthur's son, was too young to take control before the war, and sadly was lost at sea in 1944 while serving with the Royal Navy.

Enter into the Staddon story in 1946, Harold Owen White. He was born five miles away at Dunstable in 1909. His father was a Luton hat manufacturer and he could have joined the family firm, but even before he left school he had read Joseph Thorp's book 'Printing for Business' and resolved that printing was going to be his vocation. Without saying anything to his father, at the age of 15, he gained an office job with Gibbs, Bamforth & Co.,

The Bute Street Printing Works in the 1930s. (PW)

proprietors of the local newspaper 'The Luton News' and later taking a position with a London firm producing well-designed jobbing printing. In 1929 Gibbs Bamforth lured him back with a £3 a week increase, and he commenced a busy career as a local printer. In 1934 he was elected to the board, but then came the war. The Political Intelligence Department of the Foreign Office, whose country head-quarters was a few miles away at Woburn, kept him busy printing propaganda leaflets for dissemination by aircraft in enemy-occupied Europe.

After the war he and a colleague purchased the Leagrave plant of Gibbs Bamforth, renaming it The Leagrave Press. All this, so far, has nothing to do with J. Staddon & Son, but the time has come for that old-established

Harold O. White. (PW)

firm to re-enter the picture and for these two stories to become one. In 1947 The Leagrave Press bought a controlling interest, and in 1951 Harold White acquired the complete equity in his own name. In Staddons he wished to invest his love of, and interest in, printing as an art and craft. He also wanted to make more of Staddons than it had been in the past, and as he was a man who always considered his fellow human beings, he also wanted to take Staddons' old employees along with him on this joint venture. All this was achieved, the stationers progressing even more when the limited space available was increased, the printing machines having been removed to new ultra-modern buildings in Crescent Road, completed in 1956. Trading here commenced as Staddons - The Crescent Press. Eventually control of the shop was relinquished and the trading style White Crescent Press was adopted for the printing company which continued up to modern times, eventually run by his son, Peter.

As a slim schoolboy Harold had helped T.G. Hobbs carry his heavy photographic equipment, and was quietly proud of being a great-nephew of local archaeologist Worthington G. Smith. A Luton Modern School boy, he became a Justice of the Peace, Secretary of the Bedfordshire Historical Records Society and a local Rotarian. He was most proud of printing Joyce Godber's 'History of Bedfordshire' in 1969, and of founding 'The Bedfordshire Magazine' which needed vision and courage. A love of English literature led to a long friendship with George Bernard Shaw, one so close that Harold and his wife Marjorie (a daughter of Sir Herbert Janes) were witnesses to Shaw's will. It pleased Harold to publish Shaw's last work in 1950, and also with surprise and amusement to receive a

five-year subscription for the Bedfordshire Magazine from Shaw when the latter was 92!

Staddons Stationers continued until the coming of the Arndale Centre brought demolition of the Bute Street premises, but moved for a short period to 31/33 Wellington Street. H.O.White was as significant in the success of Staddons as was its namesake and founder. Dr. John Dony wrote "Few men can have had a greater love for their native town and county of their birth than Harold White".

University Cameras

A worthy description of Gruffydd Pennant Reece would be 'resolute'. Born into humble beginnings at Coedpoeth among the lead mines of North Wales where his mother taught in the local school, he was determined in all he did. Leaving home in 1933 he first gained a position with the London store Harrods as

22 Bute Street on the corner with Waller Street in 1968.

a salesman in the carpet department. He also achieved his pilot's license flying Tiger Moths at the age of 18, and wartime saw him training Battle of Britain pilots at the Elementary Flying Training School near Cambridge, achieving the rank of Flight Lieutenant. He married Nancy in 1940 and with the end of hostilities opened his first camera shop in St. Mary's Passage, Cambridge, living behind in very cramped conditions with his wife and baby daughter, Kathryn. He understandably called the shop University Cameras. With a move quite recently around the corner into Peas Hill, the premises became

Auntie's Tea Rooms and is now usually filled with tourists.

From 1946 business flourished and it was not long before they had a magnificent house on Huntingdon Road, a Daimler in the drive and a Percival Proctor at Marshall's Airport. In 1948 he bought his company to our area, opening his second premises in the vacant Trustee Savings Bank building at 22 Bute Street, at the junction with Waller Street. At this time his brother Hywel joined him, and with cousin Bryn Hyam opened the Luton shop, with its first Manager Jack Duffell who stayed only a short time. New manager Jack Hatton put the shop on the local map and I remember as a 16 years old schoolboy going with my father to buy my first quality used camera from him. He left to return to Camera House in his native Birmingham, and Lutonian Ken Batchelor became Manager. The author, who had previously been employed in "The Luton News" photographic department and also after National Service with W. H. Cox in Wellington Street, joined him in 1953, becoming Manager of the Bute Street shop in 1958 when Ken Batchelor moved to open the fourth company branch in Southampton, the third in Reading having opened a little earlier. At Head-Office the Proctor had been sold and now a boat was moored in Southampton. We noticed that Luton and Reading were in a straight line from Cambridge to Southampton, and therefore it was easy to keep an eye on us

Interior of the Bute Street shop.

do your own developing and printing and you were missing half the fun when you let someone else do it. An advertisement of 1965 suggested "Ask to see our Manager Mr. Norman. He'll be only too pleased to show you exactly what we mean by our promise- you'll make friends with photography so much more easily at University Cameras". Two well-known names who were customers at that time were Eric Morecambe to whom I remember selling projector lamps, and G. B. Shaw to whom we sent glass quarter plates for his Adams Idento camera, to his home

all whilst on the way to the boat!

In those days we were still selling Kodak Brownie box cameras, 9.5mm cine cameras and Dufaycolour and Pakolor, very early colour films, were on the shelf. Such German cameras as were available, Franka, Balda, Zeiss and the revolutionary Paxette were 'under the counter' with a waiting list for them. The odd Leica or Rolleiflex was purchased by Mr. Reece during holidays abroad and re-sold through the shop. Japanese cameras were a rarity, Miranda being among the first I recall on display. The English Purma was selling and Ken Corfield was manufacturing his unique range of British 35mm cameras. The enthusiast customers were still keen to work in their home darkrooms, or converted bathrooms, as we promoted the fact that it was much more interesting to

The author with assistant Janet Upsall in the Bute Street shop in 1956.

in Ayot St. Lawrence. We gave 16mm film shows in Stockwood House and also for the staff at Luton Hoo once a month. I was surprised on one occasion to find a guest of the Wernher family talking to me whilst I was projecting a cartoon programme for the children's Christmas party and to find

In 1955 the manager was Ken Batchelor.

that it was Douglas Fairbanks Jnr.

Bedford and Cheltenham photographic branches followed, together with audio sales departments and Fencolor Laboratory was formed in Cambridge, one of the earliest colour processing plants in the country. Nancy Reece ran a small wool shop on Kings Parade with the company offices above and yet another profitable business was in prams and toys. The Reece Group had blossomed into a very successful trading company with more than a £1M turnover with which the author stayed for 27 years, eventually becoming General Manager and personal assistant to the managing director.

Gruffydd P. Reece.

Customers, now ageing, may remember Lily Allsopp, Janet Upsall, Jenny Gallagher, and John Foster as Bute Street staff and Joe Freil was Assistant Manager for many years, later moving to open and manage the Solihull branch. The author returned to Luton when the shop was compulsorily purchased and relocated in the Arndale Centre as Bute Street was bulldozed. For six years the new shop was successful but after 31 years the company eventually left Luton in 1979, with an inability to survive the escalating costs of being at No.1 Arndale Centre. A greeting card shop found it practical for some time and it was later the premises of Tiny Computers. At time of publication it is the premises of mobile phone accessories shop Covers Galore. During the Arndale years, the author was a founder member of the Arndale Traders Association, and University Cameras in Luton was declared the Evening Post Top Shop winner in 1973.

Gruffydd Reece retired, only to build yet another enterprise. From just a dream he made the Gamlingay Vineyard in Bedfordshire a further success, planting 20,000 vines on his 10 acre property and growing and producing a new nationally accepted English wine, similar to a German Reisling. He died in 1990. Ken Batchelor enjoys retirement in West Yorkshire, Joe Freil in Lincolnshire and the author in his home town of Luton.

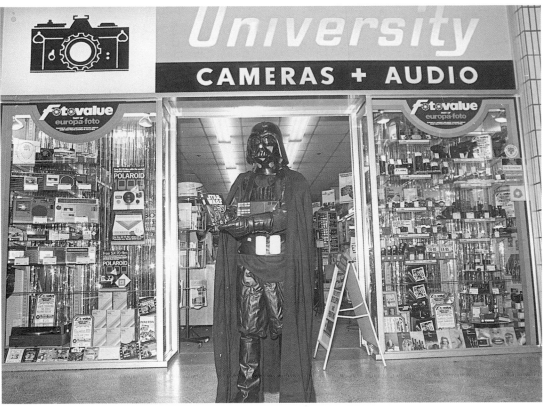

Darth Vader visits the Arndale Centre shop in 1973. (Echo & Post)

JAMES WALKER
GOLDSMITH AND SILVERSMITH LTD.

James Walker....The London Jeweller... a nationally respected name for over 150 years and one prominent in the life of Luton for over 60 years. Yet no-one knew him, for he didn't exist!

Very early in the 19th century, Sanders & Co. were noted jewellers in London, but a disagreement resulted in a family split and a new business was formed by one

48 George Street in 1959. (MD)

member of the Sanders family establishing the trading name of James Walker about 1823. The first branches were in London but later spread to the provinces, branch No.31 coming to George Street, Luton in 1926. Previously occupied by hat manufacturer A. Hucklesby, this was to become a prime position between the George Hotel Wine Stores and Woolworths, who themselves moved into the rest of the Hucklesby premises in 1933. Prominent goldsmiths, silversmiths,

jewellers and watchmakers, James Walker specialised at this time in Garrard English clocks and Elkington plate.

George Rose opened this branch and remained manager for over 30 years, living locally in Fountains Road. Noel Deeks, who lived in Tennyson Road, succeeded him in 1960, holding the position for 12 years before advancing through the company and eventually becoming joint managing director of James Walker Ltd. He is now retired. The shop was light-oak faced, and the elegant interior had counters in polished dark wood. All the showcases were of mahogany and were airtight when closed, to exclude dust and to prevent the silver from tarnishing. Like many shops in George Street and Bute Street it had only a front door, because the rear walls backed onto the George Hotel carpark. Philip Chapman, born in Luton in 1945, describes himself as Lutonian born but not bred, for he was educated at Moreton End School in Harpenden and Kent College in Canterbury. He was to become the longest serving member of Luton staff, but in 1962 he originally commenced on only a temporary basis. He served at the Hitchin branch for three years and returned to George Street as assistant manager.

Initial development of the new store for Littlewoods in 1969/70 caused problems for them at No.48 when the George Hotel was demolished, for the first floor above a number of shops in George Street comprised the hotel bedrooms. The contractors removed the upper floor, but, apparently ignorant of the fact that premises below were still in use, commenced taking off the shop ceiling. It was raining, and the ceiling began to drop! The contractors were hurriedly advised and, suitably surprised, sealed it again before closing time. Further problems arose when pile-drivers were used for the foundations. It was a busy Saturday and, with each resounding crunch, staff were kept busy catching valuable stock as it vibrated off the glass display shelves. This branch remained open until the expiry of the fifty years lease in 1976 and is now occupied by travel agents

53 Arndale Centre in 1975. (PC)

Going Places. The upper floors on this unit were never replaced and a close look shows that the present first floor is only a façade. Philip Chapman had, however, moved as manager of the new but smaller branch at 53 Arndale Centre on Smiths Square three years earlier in January 1973. A fire in the Arndale Centre in February 1976 caused hundreds of pounds worth of damage when a blaze started in the Golden Egg Restaurant. James Walker's below were counting the cost of their water-drenched premises.

The James Walker Group now comprised 135 branches, and locally made two purchases. They bought Booths China

Shop when Mona and Norman Booth reached retirement and in 1979 they purchased jewellers Edma of Luton when owner John Edelnand also retired. For all that, in 1986 they were themselves the subject of a take-over by H. Samuel who at that time had 300 branches. The valued James Walker name was retained on their premises until the early '90s, marking the end of the name in Luton after more than sixty years. Today the comprehensive Signet Group embraces the jewellery empires of H. Samuel including James Walker, Ernest Jones and Leslie Davis.

Philip Chapman, who married Avril Edwards in 1971, is still a Luton resident, and manager at H. Samuel. His hobbies are both little and large, for scale modelling came first. Now as a member of the Chiltern Vehicle Preservation Group and also the Three-Counties Bus and Commercial Vehicle Museum, he jointly owns a red single-decker London Transport bus.

Wenham and Fay Limited

Long before Mr. Block and Mr. Quayle made B. & Q. a nationally known company, the W. & F. logo was equally familiar to D.I.Y. enthusiasts in Luton, due to the marketing abilities and friendly helpful service offered by Mr. Eric Wenham and Mr. Leonard Langouroux-Fay.

Eric Wenham. (SHa)

Eric, the founder, was a Kentish Man from Tonbridge. In nearby New Romney, his grandfather had become Mayor. Father was a coal merchant whilst mother ran a general store. His twenties during WW2 were spent in the Royal Air Force, and it was his demob' at R.A.F. Cardington which brought him to Bedfordshire, where at a Bedford dance one evening he met and later married Nancy. His first job in our area was as Manager of the paint department at Frederick Gale & Co. in Bedford, later taking on the same position

Len Fay. (LF)

with Gibbs & Dandy in Cheapside, Luton. Eric's knowledge and popularity with his customers was plain to see and, ever ready to improve his lot, in 1960 he opened his first shop in Luton. This was at 47-51 Waller Street on the corner with Melson Street, and his partner in Eric Wenham Ltd. was his brother Frank.

Len Fay, for ease in business, shortened his name from that handed down from his French grandfather who lived at Ferney Voltaire very near to Lake Geneva on the French/Swiss border. Len hailed from Kilburn in London, and from the age of 14 worked at the Ascot Gas Water Heater factory which during the war was making aircraft parts. He later became a carpenter and shopfitter before meeting and marrying Valerie in 1951. It was affordable housing that brought them to Sundon Park in Luton six years later, together with a job as a maintenance fitter. He was employed by Gibbs & Dandy, and this was where he first met Eric.

At this stage Eric and his brother parted company. Frank opened his own shops in Bedford and in Park Street, Luton bearing the name Hatters. Eric was in need of a new partner, and with this in mind approached a number of business friends including myself. In 1965, however, he

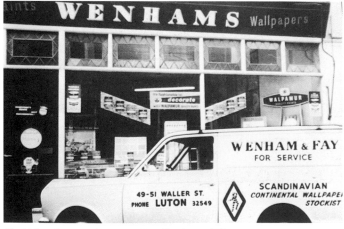

The Melson Street window at 47-51 Waller Street. (LF)

made the ideal choice, and with it the company name changed to Wenham & Fay.

Success followed and more branches were opened. La Continental in Crystal House on New Bedford Road sold only high quality wallpapers. In addition a branch was opened at 84 Wellington Street which was managed by Bill Gregory, and two more branches were opened in Bedford. The impending arrival of the Arndale Centre in Luton meant the closure of the main Waller Street branch, and a temporary move was made into Guildford Street. Later a very successful double-unit traded in the Arndale Centre, where for many years they also gave Green Shield stamps with purchases. During this time Len Fay was a founder-member of the Arndale Traders Association. In this period, following Eric Wenham's retirement, Len was joined in the business by his daughter Jan Cochrane. One may

be forgiven for thinking that a traditional family business would find it hard to compete during the rapid growth of the one-stop DIY stores. Not so in the case of Wenham & Fay, for they thrived in the Arndale Centre for the next twenty-one years, finally closing under the pressure of considerable rent increases in 1992.

Eric Wenham sadly died in 1995 following a road accident in Bedfordshire, but Len Fay still lives in Luton, enjoying his retirement caravanning and woodworking, especially making wonderfully detailed dolls houses. However, the names live on in local businesses. Len's daughter Janet manages an outlet specialising in wallpapers and carpets from a showroom in Leagrave Road, Luton. Eric's son Stuart, together with his son-in-law Peter, are factory interior designers trading as Wenham Associates.

G. A. WILD & SONS

The main form of transport in the nineteenth century was the horse, and therefore the saddler was a most important member of society at that time. None more than Ernest Wild who was the saddler in the little village of Hursley, between mid-nineteenth century in that his parents decided he should have a good education, and he must have been a bright lad, for he gained a place as a day boy at the renowned Winchester College which was eight miles away. He had to walk the sixteen miles daily, but sometimes played 'hooky' in the adjoining woods, the school

Charles E. Wild in the doorway of 14 Manchester Street in the 1920s. (SWi)

Winchester and Romsey. He was a member of a family with a history of being saddlers and wheelwrights, parish records showing the family tree back to 1665. In 1862 a son, Gilbert Ambrose, was born to Ernest and his wife, and he also was to continue in this specialised trade.

Gilbert was a fortunate lad in the eventually reporting his absence. One Monday, his Father, having business in Winchester, took him to school in the pony and trap and left him in the Headmaster's study. Business completed, Ernest returned home to report that Gilbert was safely at school. "Is he?", said his wife, "Just look in the parlour". There was Gilbert who had leapt from the Head's study and run all the way home, indeed getting there before his Father! The chance of an excellent education was wasted and the daily trek also proved too much, so he was 'put to the trade', and became, like the rest of the family, a Master Saddler.

There was insufficient work or income for all the family in the village, so 'through the trade' Ernest learned that a saddler in Luton was looking for a young journeyman saddler. So in 1885, at the age of 23, Gilbert came to Luton and joined the long-established business of Charles Ellis at 14 Manchester Street. Eventually when Mr. Ellis decided to retire, Gilbert Wild took over the business. He met and married a local girl, Clara Lawrence, and they set up home over the shop. As a sign of appreciation for all the help the previous shop owner had given them, Clara and Gilbert named their first born son Charles Ellis, who was later followed by a sister Ada Maud and younger son Sidney Gilbert. In 1910, both sons joined the company and the respected name of G.A. Wild & Sons came into being. Charles was a good sportsman, running the Luton Town Wednesday Cricket team and believing that there wasn't a local Social Club in the town of which he was not a member.

The family business was almost entirely agricultural saddlery up to and including the first world war, employing journeyman saddlers at the going wage of those days

Founder Gilbert A. Wild in 1930.

12/6d (72 ¹/₂p) to 17/6d (82¹/₂p) per week. A true story is that a market gardener brought a badly damaged saddle into the shop and asked Gilbert to repair it by the evening. When he came to collect the beautifully stitched and repaired saddle, he was told the cost was half a crown 2/6d (12¹/₂p). The customer insisted in broad Bedfordshire that he would only pay two bob (10p), which resulted in Gilbert using his half-round saddlery knife to cut through the stitches which he had painstakingly sewn on, and giving the man his saddle back. "How am I going to get home?" whined the man. "I don't know and care even less. I asked you a fair price and you refused to pay it" said Gilbert. He then added "If you want me to stitch it back it is going to cost you six shillings (30p) and I want paying first". That man never argued again.

During the Peace Day Riot in July 1919 when the Town Hall was eventually burned down, angry crowds milled around the town centre, smashing shop windows and looting. Gilbert was not going to have his shop damaged, and stood in the front porch armed with a large saddlery knife and defied the looters to come near him. The shop remained intact! With the growth of Luton and increasing industry, despite the recession, the business survived, but it was obvious to Charles and Sidney that cart harness work was declining with the advent of the van, lorry and motor car. A switch to fancy leather goods, handbags, travel and sports goods was made. Sidney went to London to learn tennis racquet stringing and repairing, whilst Charles learned the repair of cricket bats and hockey sticks.

Charles's daughter Laura, who was a hairdresser at Caspers in George Street, became at the age of 18, Beauty Queen of Skegness and was also the winner in a national contest organized by The Daily Sketch becoming Beauty Queen of Great Britain. She married racehorse owner and trainer Ron Mitchell, but within a year died of appendicitis at the age of 23. Clara Wild had died aged 74 in April 1936 and Gilbert lived for a further two years, dying in February 1938 at the age of 76. Meanwhile he had made his sons equal partners in the business. However, the next generation was also ready to continue. Charles's son Sidney came to Manchester Street from Dunstable Grammar School in 1935, but volunteered for the R.A.F. during the second world war, serving in the Middle East and Italy, and returned to the business in 1946. School supplies plus military accessories and gas mask cases created more shop work in war time. Sidney Snr's son Tony joined the business from Luton Grammar School in 1948. Gradually the emphasis

Charles E. Wild in 1955. (SWi)

changed after the war and, whilst cricket and football teams were re-formed, a lot of tennis club sites were used for housing developments and club tennis was very much reduced. The business at this stage expanded into family camping supplies as well as to enlarge into fishing tackle, toys, games and school clothing and footwear, but retaining the interest in saddlery and riding habits. The firm was supplying the Luton Town F. C. with all their kit, and one of the highlights was kitting them out for the Final of the F. A. Cup at Wembley in 1959. At this time the shop was altered and enlarged, both Sidney and Tony were made partners by their fathers, and later a limited company was formed.

When it became known that the eastern side of Manchester Street was to be demolished to create an uninterrupted view of the Central Library within the impending Arndale Centre development, a move to vast new premises in Bute Street was planned. The Manchester Street premises were vacated in 1965, which was occupied for a short time before demolition by the fabric shop Fior, and Wilds of Luton Ltd. moved into a rebuilt 8-10 Bute Street, previously the site of the premises of pawnbroker W. J. Butcher. In 1970 Tony Wild left the firm and started his own retail camping business in

Woburn Park where the business is still owned to this day by G.A. Wild - no not the founder - but Grahame Anthony, Tony's elder son who together with daughter Elizabeth (there has been an Elizabeth in the family for three hundred years) still keeps a Wild family business serving the leisure needs of the Bedfordshire public. Unfortunately the new Bute Street store did not prove financially viable and in 1972 a further move was made into the vacant Cecil Brett furniture showrooms at 12 Gordon Street. In the same year the business was sold to

Hawley Goodall who themselves remained in Luton only another six months.

Tony Wild is now living in Wadebridge, Cornwall, where Tony Wild Promotions is the U. K. agent for The Syd Lawrence Orchestra and Singers. Countrywide concerts take place, including the annual Glenn Miller Tribute Concert in Bedford Corn Exchange. Cousin Sidney, enjoying fishing and golfing in his retirement, remains in Luton, locally the last of the well-remembered Wild family who served the town for 87 years.

E. WRAY (LUTON) LTD.

In the Hertfordshire village of Breachwood Green, in 1877, Ellis Wray was born. Leaving the little school at the age of 14, he gained his first job behind the counter with Harmans in Park Street, Luton, a move being made later to similar low-paid working-class men, an ideal he never changed throughout his business life. In the opening year he took on his first assistant, Lutonian Percy Windmill, born in 1899 and also 14 when he started work was to remain with Wrays for 52 years. He married in 1926 and set up home, again over the shop, but this time above No.6 which had been added to

Left to right: Ellis Wray, Percy Windmill, Peter Windmill. (PW)

retailers Butchers in Bute Street. However, one unfortunate day, after a difference of opinion with his employer, they came to blows. Mr.Butcher ended up on the floor and Ellis Wray was unemployed!

Out of necessity, or pure ambition, or a bit of both, in 1913 he rented No.4 Castle Street next to the Red Lion Hotel, and lived over the shop. Wrays, the working man's clothier, was born. Villages such as his own birthplace were all around Luton, and they were teeming with labourers. Ellis Wray, who came from a working-class family, catered for those he knew, the

assist the expanding business. Their son Peter was born here, and the family later moved to Beresford Road. A branch in St. Albans Road, Watford, had also been opened in the early 1930's.

Crowded shop windows were the fashion at this time, and Wrays stock being large and varied it took almost an hour at opening and closing to display or remove all the items that hung outside or stood on the pavement. To make certain people could see them, they had additional exterior shopfront lighting. Percy boasted that there seemed to be nothing made that he had not at some time sold. Closing time was 7p.m. on weekdays, 9p.m. on Saturdays and midnight prior to Christmas.

With their expansion in Castle Street, and the later addition of No. 8, came a greater variety of goods for sale. There were feather beds, blankets, ticks and gramophones, field glasses, cameras, musical instruments and umbrellas. All this both new and second-hand, for they also bought for cash. The clothing sales continued of course with ready-to-wear suits from 14/11 (75p) or used ones from 8/6 (43p). You could buy moleskin trousers, teddy-lined leather motor coats

4-6 Castle Street, Luton in 1933. Left to right, Mansell Jones, Ellis Wray, Percy Windmill, William Wray. (PW)

eiderdowns. Quilts came in many colours including alambra. The carpet department offered cheap hearthrugs, peg rugs and coconut matting. There were Australian full-krome boots, hobnails and leggings. A jewellery department sold gold and silver watches and railway timekeepers, together with cutlery, sewing machines, and Bedford cord breeches. Warm underwear sold well, including stout tweed vests and fleecy-lined pants!

Ellis and his wife Nora with their two sons moved to Ludlow Avenue. Ted, the eldest, tragically lost his life in a car accident in Africa, and Gordon qualified to become a consultant anaesthetist. After 46

Ellis Wray in typical pose at his Castle Street desk in 1950. (PW)

years of business life in Castle Street, and by then aged 81, Ellis was persuaded by his wife to retire to Southbourne in 1959 where they lived until his death two years later. At this time a limited company was formed in order to ensure that progress would not be interrupted, with Mrs. Wray as Chairman of the Board. Mr Percy Windmill was appointed Managing Director with full responsibility for the running of the shops, a position he held until his retirement.

At the age of 21, Percy's son Peter Windmill had joined gents outfitters Meakers as Under-Manager of their George Street shop, and later became Manager of the Chelmsford branch. However, he returned to join his father at Wrays in 1960. Percy retired in 1965 and died seven years later. The Castle Street premises, which were owned by Miss Edith Blundell, were sold to Trust House Forte when they wanted to extend the Red Lion Hotel. Peter and his wife Christine became the sole shareholders and had to move their shop to No. 11 Upper George Street, (now part of estate agents Bradshaws). The small frontage was deceptive, for the interior extended behind 11A and in the other direction out on to Dunstable Place where Christine ran the wool shop. With foresight, when Meakers branch in Luton closed, Peter had purchased a quantity of their fixtures and fittings at a very reasonable figure, almost sufficient to refit their new Upper George Street shop. Peter is an enthusiastic amateur photographer, having served on the committee of the Luton & District Camera Club for thirty years. Retirement in Toddington came to Christine and Peter when they ended Wray's 77 years in Luton in 1990.

SUBSCRIBERS

Anne Allsopp

Jim Anderson

Doris Ballie

Malcolm Bass

Ken Batchelor

P.Bebb

Mr & Mrs N. Booth

Mrs Daphne Brown

Mr & Mrs Roy A.Brown

Bryan's Hairdressing

Elsie M.Buck

Jean & Paul Bullimore

Mrs E.Cain

Sylvia Cale (née Hodge)

Mr Alan Campbell

Challney High School for Girls

Mrs Margaret Chalmers

Alan F.Cham

Philip Chapman

Christopher Charman

Mrs Bessie Clark

J.Clark

D.Clark

Ronald Clark

Thelma Clark

Roy Cleary

Jean M. and Raymond A. Clements

Tony & Sheila Clitheroe

Ealey Conquest

Colin & Georgina Cook

Peter & Jane Cook

Irene & Stan Corin

Dr & Mrs G.P. Cotterrell

Dave Craddock

Mrs I.H.Crawley

John & Janette Croft

Peter & Patricia Crick

B.D. & S.M. Crownshaw

John & Margaret Currie

Margery Curtin

Betty Dalton

Douglas W. Dann

Anita Davidson

Vee Day

Marie & John Denman

Dr James Dyer F.S.A.

Harry Earl

John Early

Rita & John Eastwood

John S.Edelnand

Lewis & Vivienne Evans

Stuart Farmbrough

Derek Farmer

Mr & Mrs F.Fisher

Janet Foreman

Mr & Mrs J.Foster

Jennifer Gallagher

Eileen & Tony Gatward

Mr & Mrs R. Giles

J.J.M. Gillespie

Gary Gravatt

Diana Greener

Mr Tom Haines

Mr & Mrs A.J. Hales

Halyard High School

Michael F.Harrison

Jack & Audrey Harwood

Esme Hawkes

Tony & Enid Herbert

Mrs Betty Hicks

Gillian A.Hill (née Greener)

Gerry Hodge

Margaret Honey

Kelvin Hopkins M.P.

Catherine Howe

Mr M.Hubbins

Chloe Hucklesby

Dorothy Hull

Mrs Sheila Hunt

Ms Janet Hutcheon

Mrs M.Hyett
Dorothy Iszatt
Norman & Carole Jackson
Margaret James
Mr & Mrs H.G. Jarvis
R.H.Jeakings
Reg & Sylvia Joy (née Gomm)
Roy & Shirley Joyner
Alan Keene
Dorothy M. King
Mrs J.C.King
William & Mary King
Mr B.Lawrence
Mrs Jane Lawrence
Paul Lawrence
W. Lawrence
Mr L.E.L-Fay
Mrs Catherine Lindley
P.F. Lippiatt
Phyllis Luckman
T.J. & H.G. Madigan
P.Manning
Mrs F.Marsh
Nick & Margaret Marshall
Audrey V.McConnell
J.P. McIlroy
Betty McKean (née Hickman)
Lynne (née Anderson) & Tony McKee
Edna E.D. Mills
Mr A.Monks
Winnie Mooring
Mr B.A. Moss
Mr R.A. Moss
Mr R.C. Moss
Mr W.F. Moss
Mrs J. Moulsley
Mrs Mary Newman
Shirley Noller
Tony Oakey
Brian Payne
Mr & Mrs David Pell
John & Sylvia Petitt
Bill Powers
Lynda E. Powers

Mrs Sylvia Rayner
Edna Rippengale
John & Jean Robb
Norah & John Robson
Vera Robson
Andrew & Rosemary Rodell
Eileen Rodell
Rogers & Ashby (Bleachers & Dyers)
Mr C.J. Rudd
Jane A. Rust
Bill Sanders
Margaret Saunderson
Ken Severn
Betty Shaw
Malcolm H. Shaw
Geraldine Sims
M. Smith
Stuart A. Smith
Mrs Gwen Spratley
Mr E.E. Sutton
Doug Taylor
John Thompson
Alison Thursfield
Mrs Y.D. Tomkins
G. Toyer
Mrs Joan Trigg
Brenda Turnbull (née Merchant)
Christine Turner
W.L. Upton
J.C.Walker CMBHI
Richard Ward
John & Pauline Watts
Kenneth B.Webb
Bob Wells
Archie Wheewall
Wendy & David White
Tony Wild
Mr P. Windmill
Miss H.M. Wingrove
Pauline & Barry Wolsey
Christine Woodhouse (née Arnold)
M & M.P. Wooldridge
Glenys & H. Wynne-Jones
Dr G.Wray

Books Published by THE BOOK CASTLE

COUNTRYSIDE CYCLING IN BEDFORDSHIRE, BUCKINGHAMSHIRE AND HERTFORDSHIRE: Mick Payne. Twenty rides on and off-road for all the family.

PUB WALKS FROM COUNTRY STATIONS: Bedfordshire and Hertfordshire: Clive Higgs. Fourteen circular country rambles, each starting and finishing at a railway station and incorporating a pub stop at a mid way point.

PUB WALKS FROM COUNTRY STATIONS: Buckinghamshire and Oxfordshire: Clive Higgs. Circular rambles incorporating pub-stops.

LOCAL WALKS: South Bedfordshire and North Chilterns: Vaughan Basham. Twenty-seven thematic circular walks.

LOCAL WALKS: North and Mid Bedfordshire: Vaughan Basham. Twenty-five thematic circular walks.

FAMILY WALKS: Chilterns South: Nick Moon. Thirty 3 to 5 mile circular walks.

FAMILY WALKS: Chilterns North: Nick Moon. Thirty shorter circular walks.

CHILTERN WALKS: Hertfordshire, Bedfordshire and North Bucks: Nick Moon.

CHILTERN WALKS: Buckinghamshire: Nick Moon.

CHILTERN WALKS: Oxfordshire and West Buckinghamshire: Nick Moon. A trilogy of circular walks, in association with the Chiltern Society. Each volume contains 30 circular walks.

OXFORDSHIRE WALKS: Oxford, the Cotswolds and the Cherwell Valley: Nick Moon.

OXFORDSHIRE WALKS: Oxford, the Downs and the Thames Valley: Nick Moon. Two volumes that complement Chiltern Walks: Oxfordshire, and complete coverage of the county, in association with the Oxford Fieldpaths Society. Thirty circular walks in each.

THE D'ARCY DALTON WAY: Nick Moon. Long-distance footpath across the Oxfordshire Cotswolds and Thames Valley, with various circular walk suggestions.

THE CHILTERN WAY: Nick Moon. A guide to the new 133 mile circular Long-Distance Path through Bedfordshire, Buckinghamshire, Hertfordshire and Oxfordshire, as planned by the Chiltern Society.

CHANGES IN OUR LANDSCAPE: Aspects of Bedfordshire, Buckinghamshire and the Chilterns 1947-1992: Eric Meadows. Over 350 photographs from the author's collection spanning nearly 50 years.

JOURNEYS INTO BEDFORDSHIRE: Anthony Mackay. Foreword by The Marquess of Tavistock, Woburn Abbey. A lavish book of over 150 evocative ink drawings.

COCKNEY KID & COUNTRYMEN: Ted Enever. The Second World War remembered by the children of Woburn Sands and Aspley Guise. A six year old boy is evacuated from London's East End to start life in a Buckinghamshire village.

CHANGING FACES, CHANGING PLACES: Post war Bletchley and Woburn Sands 1945-1970: Ted Enever. Evocative memoirs of post-war life on the Beds/Bucks borders, up to the coming of Milton Keynes new town.

BUCKINGHAM AT WAR: Pip Brimson. Stories of courage, humour and pathos as Buckingham people adapt to war.

WINGS OVER WING: The Story of a World War II Bomber Training Unit: Mike Warth. The activities of RAF Wing in Buckinghamshire.

JOURNEYS INTO BUCKINGHAMSHIRE: Anthony Mackay. Superb line drawings plus background text: large format landscape gift book.

BUCKINGHAMSHIRE MURDERS: Len Woodley. Nearly two centuries of nasty crimes.

WINGRAVE: A Rothschild Village in the Vale: Margaret and Ken Morley. Thoroughly researched and copiously illustrated survey of the last 200 years in this lovely village between Aylesbury and Leighton Buzzard.

HISTORIC FIGURES IN THE BUCKINGHAMSHIRE LANDSCAPE: John Houghton. Major personalities and events that have shaped the county's past, including Bletchley Park.

TWICE UPON A TIME: John Houghton. North Bucks short stories loosely based on fact.

SANCTITY AND SCANDAL IN BEDS AND BUCKS: John Houghton. A miscellany of unholy people and events.

MANORS and MAYHEM, PAUPERS and PARSONS: Tales from Four Shires: Beds., Bucks., Herts. and Northants: John Houghton. Little known historical snippets and stories.

THE LAST PATROL: Policemen killed on duty while serving the Thames Valley: Len Woodley.

FOLK: Characters and Events in the History of Bedfordshire and Northamptonshire: Vivienne Evans. Anthology of people of yesteryear -arranged alphabetically by village or town.

JOHN BUNYAN: His Life and Times: Vivienne Evans. Highly praised and readable account.

THE RAILWAY AGE IN BEDFORDSHIRE: Fred Cockman. Classic, illustrated account of early railway history.

A LASTING IMPRESSION: Michael Dundrow. A boyhood evacuee recalls his years in the Chiltern village of Totternhoe near Dunstable.

ELEPHANTS I'LL NEVER FORGET: A Keeper's Life at Whipsnade and London Zoo: John Weatherhead. Experiences, dramatic and sad, from a lifetime with these well-loved giants.

WHIPSNADE MY AFRICA: Lucy Pendar. The inside story of sixty years of this world-renowned institution. Full of history, anecdotes, stories of animals and people.

GLEANINGS REVISITED: Nostalgic Thoughts of a Bedfordshire Farmer's Boy: E.W. O'Dell. His own sketches and early photographs adorn this lively account of rural Bedfordshire in days gone by.

BEDFORDSHIRE'S YESTERYEARS: The Rural Scene: Brenda Fraser-Newstead. Vivid first-hand accounts of country life two or three generations ago.

BEDFORDSHIRE'S YESTERYEARS: Craftsmen and Tradespeople: Brenda Fraser-Newstead. Fascinating recollections over several generations practising many vanishing crafts and trades.

BEDFORDSHIRE'S YESTERYEARS: War Times and Civil Matters: Brenda Fraser-Newstead. Two World Wars, plus transport, law and order, etc.

DUNNO'S ORIGINALS: A facsimile of the rare pre-Victorian history of Dunstable and surrounding villages. New preface and glossary by John Buckledee, Editor of The Dunstable Gazette.

DUNSTABLE DOWN THE AGES: Joan Schneider and Vivienne Evans. Succinct overview of the town's prehistory and history - suitable for all ages.

HISTORIC INNS OF DUNSTABLE: Vivienne Evans. Illustrated booklet, especially featuring ten pubs in the town centre.

EXPLORING HISTORY ALL AROUND: Vivienne Evans. Planned as seven circular car tours, plus background to places of interest en-route in Bedfordshire and parts of Bucks and Herts.

PROUD HERITAGE: A Brief History of Dunstable, 1000-2000AD: Vivienne Evans. Century by century account of the town's rich tradition and key events, many of national significance.

DUNSTABLE WITH THE PRIORY: 1100-1550: Vivienne Evans. Dramatic growth of Henry I's important new town around a major crossroads.

DUNSTABLE IN TRANSITION: 1550-1700: Vivienne Evans. Wealth of original material as the town evolves without the Priory.

DUNSTABLE DECADE: THE EIGHTIES: A Collection of Photographs: Pat Lovering. A souvenir book of nearly 300 pictures of people and events in the 1980's

STREETS AHEAD: An Illustrated Guide to the Origins of Dunstable's Street Names: Richard Walden. Fascinating text and captions to hundreds of photographs, past and present, throughout the town.

DUNSTABLE IN DETAIL: Nigel Benson. A hundred of the town's buildings and features, plus town trail map.

DUNSTAPLE: A Tale of The Watling Highway: A.W. Mooring. Dramatic novelisation of Dunstable's legend of Dunne the Robber - reprinted after a century out of print.

25 YEARS OF DUNSTABLE: Bruce Turvey. Reissue of this photographic treasure-trove of the town up to the Queen's Silver Jubilee, 1952-77.

DUNSTABLE SCHOOL: 1888-1971. F.M. Bancroft. Short history of one of the town's most influential institutions.

BOURNE and BRED: A Dunstable Boyhood Between the Wars: Colin Bourne. An elegantly written, well illustrated book capturing the spirit of the town over fifty years ago.

OLD HOUGHTON: Pat Lovering. Pictorial record capturing the changing appearances of Houghton Regis over the past 100 years.

ROYAL HOUGHTON: Pat Lovering. Illustrated history of Houghton Regis from the earliest of times to the present.

WERE YOU BEING SERVED?: Remembering 50 Luton Shops of Yesteryear: Bob Norman. Well-illustrated review of the much loved, specialist outlets of a generation or two ago.

A BRAND NEW BRIGHT TOMORROW... A Hatters Promotion Diary: Caroline Dunn. A fans account of Luton Town Football Club during the 2001-2002 season.

GIRLS IN BLUE: Christine Turner. The activities of the famous Luton Girls Choir properly documented over its 41 year period from 1936 to 1977.

THE STOPSLEY BOOK: James Dyer. Definitive, detailed account of this historic area of Luton. 150 rare photographs.

THE STOPSLEY PICTURE BOOK: James Dyer. New material and photographs make an ideal companion to The Stopsley Book.

PUBS and PINTS: The Story of Luton's Public Houses and Breweries: Stuart Smith. The background to beer in the town, plus hundreds of photographs, old and new.

LUTON AT WAR - VOLUME ONE: As compiled by the Luton News in 1947, a well illustrated thematic account.

LUTON AT WAR - VOLUME TWO: Second part of the book compiled by The Luton News.

THE CHANGING FACE OF LUTON: An Illustrated History: Stephen Bunker, Robin Holgate and Marian Nichols. Luton's development from earliest times to the present busy industrial town. Illustrated in colour and mono.

WHERE THEY BURNT THE TOWN HALL DOWN: Luton, The First World War and the Peace Day Riots, July 1919: Dave Craddock. Detailed analysis of a notorious incident.

THE MEN WHO WORE STRAW HELMETS: Policing Luton, 1840-1974: Tom Madigan. Fine chronicled history, many rare photographs; author~served in Luton Police for fifty years.

BETWEEN THE HILLS: The Story of Lilley, a Chiltern Village: Roy Pinnock. A priceless piece of our heritage - the rural beauty remains but the customs and way of life described here have largely disappeared.

KENILWORTH SUNSET: A Luton Town Supporter's Journal: Tim Kingston. Frank and funny account of football's ups and downs.

A HATTER GOES MAD!: Kristina Howells. Luton Town footballers, officials and supporters talk to a female fan.

LEGACIES: Tales and Legends of Luton and the North Chilterns: Vic Lea. Mysteries and stories based on fact, including Luton Town Football Club. Many photographs.

THREADS OF TIME: Shela Porter. The life of a remarkable mother and business-woman, spanning the entire century and based in Hitchin and (mainly) Bedford.

FARM OF MY CHILDHOOD, 1925-1947: Mary Roberts. An almost vanished lifestyle on a remote farm near Flitwick.

STICKS AND STONES: The Life and Times of a Journeyman Printer in Hertford, Dunstable, Cheltenham and Wolverton: Harry Edwards.

CRIME IN HERTFORDSHIRE Volume 1 Law and Disorder: Simon Walker. Authoritative, detailed survey of the changing legal process over many centuries.

JOURNEYS INTO HERTFORDSHIRE: Anthony Mackay. A foreword by The Marquis of Salisbury, Hatfield House. Introducing nearly 200 superbly detailed line drawings.

LEAFING THROUGH LITERATURE: Writers' Lives in Herts and Beds: David Carroll. Illustrated short biographies of many famous authors and their connections with these counties.

A PILGRIMAGE IN HERTFORDSHIRE: H.M. Alderman. Classic, between-the-wars tour round the county, embellished with line drawings.

THE VALE OF THE NIGHTINGALE: Molly Andrews. Several generations of a family, lived against a Harpenden backdrop.

SUGAR MICE AND STICKLEBACKS: Childhood Memories of a Hertfordshire Lad: HarryEdwards.Vivid evocation of gentle pre-war in an archetypal village, Hertingfordbury.

SWANS IN MY KITCHEN: Lis Dorer. Story of a Swan Sanctuary near Hemel Hempstead.

MYSTERIOUS RUINS: The Story of Sopwell, St. Albans: Donald Pelletier. Still one of the town's most atmospheric sites. Sopwell's history is full of fluctuations and interest, mainly as a nunnery associated with St. Albans Abbey.

THE HILL OF THE MARTYR: An Architectural History of St. Albans Abbey: Eileen Roberts. Scholarly and readable chronological narrative history of Hertfordshire and Bedfordshire's famous cathedral. Fully illustrated with photographs and plans.

THE TALL HITCHIN INSPECTOR'S CASEBOOK: A Victorian Crime Novel Based on Fact: Edgar Newman. Worthies of the time encounter more archetypal villains.

SPECIALLY FOR CHILDREN

VILLA BELOW THE KNOLLS: A Story of Roman Britain: Michael Dundrow.
An exciting adventure for young John in Totternhoe and Dunstable two thousand years ago.

THE RAVENS: One Boy Against the Might of Rome: James Dyer. On the Barton Hills and in the south-east of England as the men of the great fort of Ravensburgh (near Hexton) confront the invaders.

TITLES ACQUIRED BY THE BOOK CASTLE

BEDFORDSHIRE WILDLIFE: B.S. Nau, C.R. Boon, J.P. Knowles for the Bedfordshire Natural History Society. Over 200 illustrations, maps, photographs and tables survey the plants and animals of this varied habitat.

BIRDS OF BEDFORDSHIRE: Paul Trodd and David Kramer. Environments, breeding maps and details of 267 species, with dozens of photographs, illustrations and diagrams.

A BEDFORDSHIRE QUIZ BOOK: Eric G. Meadows. Wide ranging quizzes and picture puzzles on the history, people, places and bygones of the county.

CURIOSITIES OF BEDFORDSHIRE: A County Guide to the Unusual: Pieter and Rita Boogaart. Quirky, well-illustrated survey of little-known features throughout the county.

THE BIRDS OF HERTFORDSHIRE: Tom Gladwin and Bryan Sage. Essays, maps and records for all 297 species, plus illustrations, photographs and other plates.

BUTTERFLIES OF HERTFORDSHIRE: Brian Sawford. History and ecological guide, with colour photographs and maps for nearly 50 species.

WELWYN RAILWAYS: Tom Gladwin, Peter Neville, Douglas White. A history of the Great Northern line from 1850 to 1986, as epitomised by the five mile stretch between Welwyn Garden City and Woolmer Green. Profusely illustrated in colour and black and white - landscape format.

LIFE AND TIMES OF THE GREAT EASTERN RAILWAY (1839-1922): Harry Paar and Adrian Gray. Personalities, accidents, traffic and tales, plus contemporary photographs and old o.s. maps of this charming railway that transformed East Anglia and Hertfordshire between 1839 and 1922.

THE QUACK: Edgar Newman. Imaginative faction featuring characters in a nineteenth-century painting of a busy Hitchin market scene - especially quack doctor William Mansell.

D-DAY TO ARNHEIM - with Hertfordshire's Gunners: Major Robert Kiln. Vivid, personal accounts of the D-Day preparations and drama, and the subsequent Normandy battles, plus photographs and detailed campaign maps.

THE BOOK CASTLE
12 Church Street, Dunstable
Bedfordshire LU5 4RU
Tel: (01582) 605670 Fax (01582) 662431
Email: bc@book-castle.co.uk
Website: www.book-castle.co.uk

A BRAND NEW BRIGHT TOMORROW...
A Hatter's Promotion Diary
by Caroline Dunn

It's a roller-coaster ride being a Luton fan. The one certain thing when you're following the Town is that it'll never be boring.

Follow Caroline Dunn on the Hatter's journey back up to the Second Division, during one of the most exciting seasons in living memory. Villains turned to heroes as the Town completed 2001-2002 with a record breaking run, sealing promotion and netting one hundred goals over the course of the season. Travelogues, match reports and conversations with the players are all included - as well as a certain amount of smugness from the woman who said at the start of the season that Steve Howard, winner of the Divisional Golden Boot, would come good.

From Carlisle to Cheltenham, Darlington to Dagenham, this is a diary of ten marvellous months in the life of a supporter.

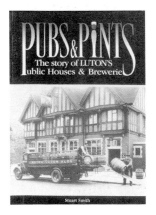

PUBS AND PINTS
The Story of Luton's Public Houses and Breweries
Stuart Smith

Whilst the town of Luton is well documented in other ways, this profusely illustrated book is the first comprehensive history of its important brewing industry and retail beer outlets-linked, staple trades in the area for over five hundred years.

The development of the modern public house from the early taverns and coaching inns closely followed that of the breweries, with the final decades of the last century seen as the high point in the number of houses licensed to sell beers for consumption on or off the premises. Since then the total has declined with the loss of around 40% during the last one hundred years, most of these losses occurring in the period from 1950 to 1970.

Although written documentation dealing with the early breweries and public houses is extremely sparse, it is the intention of this book to try to record the history of each brewery and public house that has had a bearing on the social and drinking pastimes of Lutonians over the last one hundred and fifty years. Similarly a special feature of the book is the vast range of three hundred representative photographs- many old, rare and unusual.

The Book Castle

THE CHANGING FACE OF LUTON
Stephen Bunker, Robin Holgate & Marian Nichols

"The Changing Face of Luton" traces the fortunes of the settlement and economy of the town from the earliest recorded arrival of people in the area to the present day. It looks at different aspects of Luton and its development rather than giving a straight chronological account of its history.

Luton's roots go back a very long way, yet in less than 200 years it has changed from a small market town to today's busy industrial and commercial centre. This transformation is described, helped by a range of excellent photographs, thereby answering many of the questions frequently asked, and perhaps raising more, about this intriguing town.

The three authors from Luton Museum are all experts in local history, archaeology and industry.

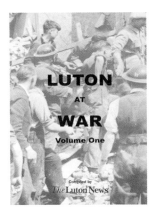

LUTON AT WAR
VOLUME ONE & VOLUME TWO

Initially published by the Luton News in 1947, the story of how the people of Luton withstood the dark years of war between 1939 and 1945.

Because of strict war-time censorship much of what occurred during those years was not mentioned in The Luton News. Once the war was over however, The Luton News set about the mammoth task of presenting a complete and vivid picture of war-time life. It tells of the long anxious nights, the joy and the sorrow that made even the most terrifying moments bearable thanks to the tremendous way in which the people joined to help each other.

Written and compiled by the staff of The Luton News at the time, it contains the most comprehensive and fascinating pictorial record. As well as being a moving personal account it is a unique historical document.

Now published in large format paperback in two parts, it is packed with hundreds of rare photographs. For this edition, a new index has been compiled by James Dyer, appearing in the second book but covering both volumes.

GIRLS IN BLUE
The Story of the Luton Girls Choir
by Christine Turner

Girls in Blue recounts the story of the unique musical phenomenon that was the Luton Girls Choir. Founded in 1936, it became internationally famous, performing for 41 years until the death of its founder and musical director Arthur Davies.

The author, Christine Turner, felt that it was time that the activities of the Choir were properly documented and gathered her information by meeting many former members of the Choir and sharing their memories as well as enjoying the search through the many scrapbooks, newspaper cuttings and programmes left by Mr Davies.